Knits About Winter
Published in 2018 by Pom Pom Press
Text, Illustrations, and Photography © 2018 Emily Foden

All rights reserved. No portion of this book may be reproduced or transmitted in any form or by any means, mechanical, electronically, photocopying, recording, or otherwise, without written permission of the publisher. For personal use only.
ISBN: 978-0-9934866-8-5
A catalogue record for this book is available from the British Library.
pompommag.com

Photography: Emily Foden
Editors: Meghan Fernandes & Lydia Gluck
Managing Editor: Amy Collins
Media Manager: Sophie Scott
Design & Layout: Murray Wyse
Technical Editors: Laura Chau & Jemima Bicknell
Copy Editors: Annie Prime & Francesca Baldry
Models: Kiyomi & Sachiko Burgin
Sample Knitters: Kiyomi Burgin (Eastwind), Natalie Selles (Winterberry & Favourite Socks version 4), Susie Vuyanovich (Soirée Mooresburg DK version), Christine de Boer (Soirée, light version)
Locations: The Stutzman family farm (Snowy fields, sleigh ride & horses), Skyhill (forest sunset), Black Sheep Farm (barn & sheep)
Jewellery Provided by Hedgling (Sachiko Burgin)
With thanks to Phaedra Clothing for the green jumpsuit styled with Soirée & Pyne & Smith Clothiers for checked and striped dresses styled with Snowshoe and Winterberry.

For pattern corrections, please visit:
pompommag.com/errata

Printed in the UK by Pureprint Group Limited

POM POM PRESS
C005 Lighthouse Space
89A Shacklewell Lane
London E8 2EB
United Kingdom

pompommag.com
violaandthemoon.com

This book is dedicated to the inhabitants of Mooresburg past, present, and future.

contents

008
Foreword

010
Introduction

014
Winter in Mooresburg

016
Behind the Scenes at Viola

024
The Patterns

026
Eastwind

036
Snowdrift

044
Snowshoe

050
Skyhill

058
Barn

066
Full Moon

074
Persephone

082
Mitten Liners

086
Soirée

094
Winterberry

102
Frost

112
Favourite Socks

120
Creating the Colourways

132
Acknowledgements

133
Abbreviations

A download code for the digital edition of this book can be found on the inside of the back cover.

foreword

We first encountered Emily Foden's magical way with dyeing yarn when we worked in the knitting shop Loop, in London. Sold under the name Viola, each skein was perfectly imperfect, not to mention unique, with tiny splashes of colour. Whenever a new shipment came in we would covet *that* specific dye lot of yarn. Who knew when we'd see another skein like it? These were the heady first days of the hand-dyed yarn renaissance, if you will, and perhaps even before it was widely desirable for skeins not to be identical. But Emily's yarns had captured our imaginations.

We knew very little about Emily at that time. Once in a blue moon, a large, heavy box would arrive from Canada, with a playfully handwritten address, full of glowing skeins. The labels often changed, and it was exciting to see what lovely doodle would appear on the tags next. These batches of yarn were like gold dust - in the shop one morning, and then out by the following week. Then we heard that Emily would be moving to England. We were excited and intrigued that she had decided to move to Devon in the southwest of the country, to work with and learn from John Arbon, whose mill is renowned for producing some of the UK's finest wool yarns. To our delight, during her stay in the UK Emily became both a good friend and a contributor to Pom Pom.

It was during the photo shoot for our 5th anniversary issue, to which Emily had contributed a design in her yarn, that it occurred to us that her work as a yarn dyer, pattern designer, and illustrator would make for a beautiful book.

We are honoured that Emily agreed to make this book with us, and that she welcomed us into her home, studio, and the tiny hamlet of Mooresburg where she lives, and which inspired the colours and designs in this book. We hope that it encourages you to find the beauty and colour in winter, and helps you to welcome the coldest, darkest season with the warm glow that we still feel from being a part of its creation.

Meghan Fernandes & Lydia Gluck
October 2018

introduction

I moved to an old general store at the beginning of a very cold and snowy winter in 2015. A century ago, Mooresburg was a bustling little hamlet, but it is now a quiet crossroads surrounded by fields and forest. My move to the country coincided with my return to Canada after living in England for three years.

This was a big change in itself, and one I was reluctant to make at the time. I felt uprooted, directionless and uncertain about almost everything. Although I didn't realise it at the time, I spent that winter mapping out the course of the next few years of my life, and my business, Viola Yarns. I went on long walks, taking in my new surroundings and the winter landscape. I made time for drawing, painting, knitting and baking. I know how fortunate I was to have had that time and freedom, and certainly haven't found much spare time since! I remember that beautiful winter vividly, and am certain that the quiet, stillness and solitude of those months was exactly what I needed in order to rest, recuperate and take my next steps forward when spring arrived. Winter in Mooresburg has been an invaluable source of inspiration ever since.

Winter is quiet in so many ways: humans and wildlife alike prefer to remain sheltered and warm, hibernating the coldest months away while snow absorbs what little sound remains outside. Layer upon layer of snow transforms the ordinary world and landscape into a dreamworld, a sparkling blank canvas for the mind and imagination. Frozen rivers, lakes and ponds provide rare access to parts of the landscape that are out of reach in warmer seasons, and if walking on a river doesn't sound magical, I don't know what does! Sunrise and sunset's warm blaze of orange and pink reflects in falling snow, frost and ice, filling the air with a soft pastel haze. I love nothing more than to bundle up and stomp off through the snow, exploring the frozen world outside, following footprints through the woods and studying frost in the trees. I love feeling like I'm the only one for miles, even though a silent-footed deer is likely to be staring right at me. It's the distance that winter provides from the rest of the busy world that allows me to recentre, focus and make good decisions.

Introduction

Three years later, Viola and I are up and running in the Mooresburg general store, and snow is falling outside my window. Viola has grown and changed continually since I moved back to Canada, and I have learned so much from the hard work that went along with that growth. I have become well acquainted with the challenges of balancing work and life, and how the lines often blur and work takes over completely. Without the luxury of the whole winter to ponder and plan, I am slowly learning how to separate my mind from work for little snippets of time. Those moments of quiet and distance, in turn, help to keep me on course. Winter stops my mind from its constant churning. For once there are no words. Just quiet.

Without sounding too grim, I must speak briefly about the challenges of winter, and how they have also influenced this book. As a city dweller, my day-to-day experience of winter had been somewhat removed before I moved to Mooresburg. I would watch snowfall from inside the house, and grumble about ankle-deep slush as I struggled to walk down the street. There is something about living in an old building that has brought history into my daily life, and in my short time here I have learned about the former inhabitants of the general store as well as the hamlet of Mooresburg. Their winters were not as easy as mine. Average snowfall was greater 100 years ago, occasionally reaching telephone pole height, yet ploughs were fewer. Horses broke trails through the snow and men with shovels cleared what little they could by hand. Heating homes with wood in minus 40°C would have been a neverending task, there were no down coats to slip on for the buggy ride into town, and it was a long, cold trek to the outhouse. These hard-working and seriously tough people survived harsh winters, and I often think of them on my winter explorations. What did they see in the snow, forest and sky? Perhaps the same magic that I see now, or maybe just the long, hard months ahead? Whatever their thoughts may have been, they remind me that winter is also dangerous. As much as I might like to wander about in the forest all winter, I would certainly freeze to death if I stayed out too long. I have a great deal of respect and admiration for the previous inhabitants of Mooresburg, and I have kept them in my mind throughout my work and in my daily life in the store.

This book is inspired by my experiences of winter in Mooresburg, but I believe that I am describing characteristics of winter that are shared wherever there is a cold and dark season of snow. This place is special to me, because it is where I first experienced the magic of winter as I've described it. I have come to think of winter as two opposing factors: a magical, quiet internal space in a harsh, dangerous landscape. I am lucky enough to live in a time when I do not fear freezing to death, but I have great respect for winter's power – and necessity. I look forward to the quiet time for contemplation, creativity and exploration, and I never take for granted the wild magic that is always just

slightly out of reach. I realise that my deep love of winter places me in a rare minority of the human population, and am perfectly happy with that. Summer lovers, I invite you to bundle up by the fire, perhaps knit some of the projects in this book and enjoy my favourite things about winter from the cosy comfort of your home. I'll see you again in spring!

winters in Mooresburg

Even though I have lived in Mooresburg for over three years, I still feel like the new kid on the block.

I am often asked about my 'new' home, why I chose to live here and what I make of it. No matter what my answer, I always end up at the realisation that Mooresburg is quite the bustling place to be. I did not expect this to be the case.

While a passing tractor may be the only traffic for hours, under the surface is a tightly connected community with a constant buzz of activity. Dances, farm auctions, meat rolls (I still do not completely understand what this is, but am told that it's lots of fun), stag and doe parties, barn raisings, bonfires, fishing trips, weddings, funerals, farmer's markets, motor-free parades… I think you get the picture. There is rarely a dull moment in Mooresburg.

My adventures while settling into this new home haven't slowed down at all during winter, despite the quiet and solitude of the season. As much as I would like to spend all of my time in a wintery dreamland, I have to face reality from time to time. Tasks like shovelling snow, chipping ice from car windscreens and battling frozen pipes are usually a source of stress and anxiety for most people. I admit that I was not exactly happy or calm when the pipes froze in my dye studio this winter, although an overflowing sink froze into a rather amazing waterfall of ice which then created a little frozen pond on the studio floor. Water filters cracked and burst and all dyeing ground to a halt for a few cold months. As I say, the adventures never cease.

There was the time I jammed a snowshoe under three feet of snow, somehow hooking it under a fallen tree. I spent a few panicked moments in a distorted split lunge over a snowdrift, but eventually wriggled free laughing. Last winter a bear awoke from its hibernation and was wandering the neighbourhood in search of food. I never laid eyes on it, but passed some alarmingly large prints in the snow. My dog Lucy caught its scent and wisely retreated into the house. She's not a risk-taker! The snow ploughs have their work cut out for them here, and usually pass through Mooresburg between three and six in the morning. In addition to a reliably early wake-up call, shovelling out the densely packed snow deposited by the plough is an adventure to say the least.

Wise locals have learned not to risk driving on bad days. Blowing snow creates huge slippery drifts across the road and makes visibility very poor. My friends at Skyhill nearby have a famously treacherous driveway, which curves up a steep slope. I haven't got properly stuck yet, but have pushed my car out of the bank a few times, only to reverse dubiously back down the hill the way I came.

The woodstove is the centre of indoor life as distant corners of the draughty store become too cold to venture into. My yoga practice moves into the kitchen, and a hat and socks must be worn to bed. Each morning in the studio, ice has formed in my dye pots and snow has snuck in through cracks in the door.

I love the adventures that winter provides; while they can be stressful and time consuming, they are also a rather exciting feature of the season. The work of staying warm, dry and cosy is ongoing, but so satisfying. I think most of us agree that being cosy is a wonderful feeling, and we would take it for granted without the challenges of the cold.

behind the scenes at Viola

When I returned to Canada from the UK, I wasn't sure whether I wanted to dye yarn again. I had been away for such a long time and much had changed in my life as well as in the world of knitting. I had a very long list of dreams, plans and projects that I hoped to embark on, and I thought perhaps the time had come for something new. As with most of the heavy decisions I've made in life, I drifted back into dyeing yarn without realising what I was doing. Four years after my return to Canada, I have never looked back or second-guessed that non-decision, but I still have that list of dreams ready and waiting for somewhere down the road.

During my years in England, my parents' search for a new place to call home ultimately brought them to Mooresburg. Grey County was a part of Ontario that was unfamiliar to us all, but the lure of a creaky old disused general store was irresistible. By the time I returned to Canada, they had bought 'the store', as we like to call it, and were dividing their time between Toronto and Mooresburg.

It turns out that the store is quite a famous local building. Its distinctive cedar shakes and bright red roof certainly stand out from the little cluster of homes that make up Mooresburg today. It has not operated as a store since the 1970s, but neighbours can remember buying candy or returning empty bottles there. The building has changed over the years but still has a dirt floor in the basement and a storefront on the ground floor with original wooden shelves that run floor to ceiling and are now full of yarn. We know these shelves once held items like Salada Tea because faded price stickers remain in some places. Only a few locals recall the legendary oak counter that ran the length of the store, yet it is highly revered. Upstairs, the bedrooms have amazingly high ceilings and above them is an attic that

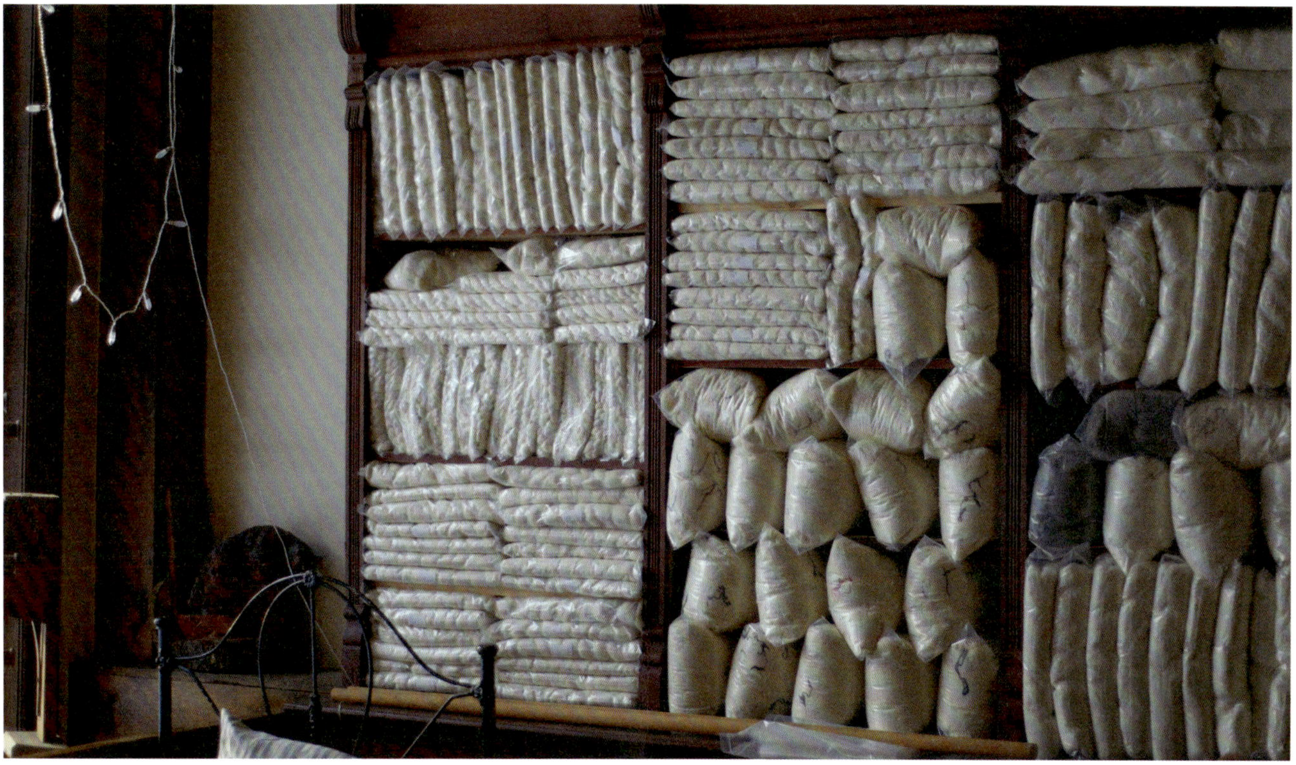

These instructions use 10gm of dye powder and will dye 1kg of fibre.
Soak fibre in warm water for 20

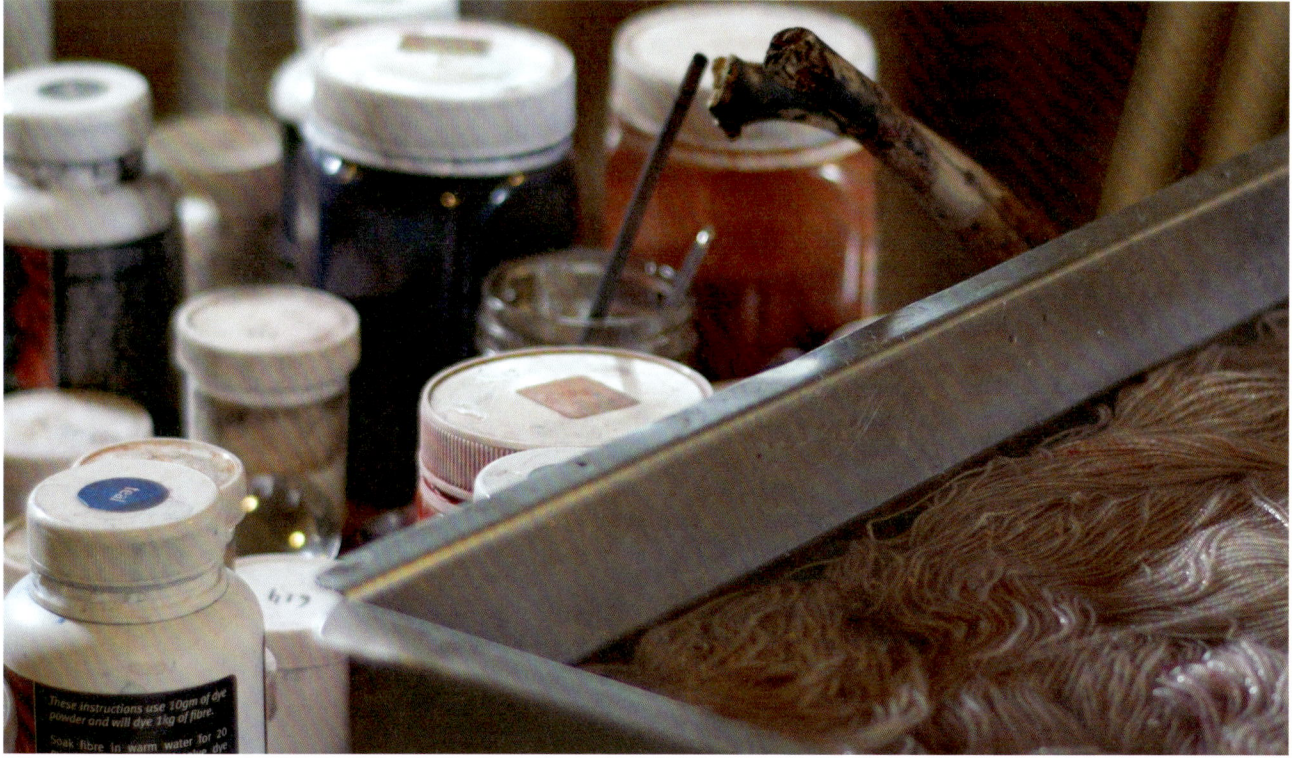

Behind the Scenes at Viola

is very popular with bats. The building has been used by the community since it was built over 100 years ago: apparently dances were held upstairs; snow plough drivers stopped in to warm themselves by the fire on cold winter nights; and the dance hall doubled as lodgings for mill workers from time to time. The store used to house the post office as well as gas pumps and even won a window display contest back in the 1930s. Many families have lived in the building and run the store. Some rented and some owned; each made changes and left their mark.

When the store was built in 1896, the village of Mooresburg was much busier than it is now. Land in the area had been cleared for farming through the backbreaking labour of settlers and horses who found themselves in swamps and forests teeming with black flies and mosquitos. Large areas of old-growth forest were cleared for farming and their precious trees were so abundant that they had to be burned in order to slowly clear the land. Settlers from the UK and Europe were not equipped for the long, cold winters and many simply froze to death in their little cabins. At one time or another there has been a church, blacksmith shop, sawmill and even a rival store in Mooresburg. Farms are dotted farther afield along with ponds, rivers, swamps, and lakes. Tiny one-room school houses are on almost every corner while the remnants of mills, maple syrup shacks, and little pockets of old-growth forest hang on in some areas.

Today it often feels as though I live and work in a museum. This building has been an important part of so many lives and families, and we are often reminded of that fact when people appear at our door with memories, stories, and photographs of the store throughout the years. This building still brings people together to share information, news, and memories, although we have no plans to host another dance upstairs!

When I found myself back in Canada, relocating to this new space felt like the most natural thing to do. During my time in North Devon, I drifted far away from city life. I came back to Canada craving open space, fresh air, and nature over the noise and crowds of the city. I love to visit cities now and enjoy them even more as a visitor than I did as an inhabitant. I seek out galleries, knitting stores, and tasty food, but am always delighted to return to my quiet home and visit my favourite trees. My move to Mooresburg came about through two big changes that happened more or less at the same time: leaving England and leaving Toronto. As a result I took a little adjustment period when I first arrived. More than settling into the new space, I needed to come to terms with the people and things I had left behind.

It wasn't long before I was planning to set up a dye studio in Mooresburg, launch a Kickstarter campaign to fund the renovations and organise a great big party to thank everyone involved. Luckily

for me, I am surrounded by resourceful, hardworking, and capable people who helped with every stage of the process. My studio space is in a converted side shed attached to the main store. It would have been used for extra store merchandise, and our visitors have corroborated that potatoes and shovels were stored in there at one time or another. The shed originally had an earth floor and flimsy outer walls. It was full of many years' worth of accumulated gardening items and its horror film-esque door to the basement was foamed shut to prevent animal intruders.

Friends, new and old, lent their time and skills installing vents, windows and cement floors. We dug out the earth floor on the hottest day of summer 2016, unearthing deer bones, rusted shears, and other little treasures. The walls were covered with spray foam insulation and pine boards from a local sawmill. Electricity and plumbing had to be installed, and sinks, stoves, and lights purchased. Eventually I even faced my fears of the basement and got that scary door open.

The Kickstarter campaign was a greater success than I could have ever imagined. I set my target amount at $5,000, hoping to offset some of the building costs. Being clueless about renovation, I had grossly underestimated what those costs would be. When the campaign closed at $15,000 I spent a week or two in shock before springing into action with rewards. I was riding high on the surprise success of the campaign and dyeing yarn day and night in order to send out rewards on time. Ironically, the renovations had to be put on hold until I had finished. I was struck by the generosity and support of the backers. Even though I had disappeared for three years, they were right there when I returned, not only with financial support through Kickstarter, but also with messages of encouragement.

The excitement of Kickstarter flowed straight into planning a party. We chose to host it in autumn to minimise the amount of biting insects and to ensure proper sweater weather. Friends came from near and far to celebrate. A fantastic dance party was safely located on the main floor. It felt as though the old building enjoyed having happy crowds of people using its rooms again. It was the old store as it was meant to be: a space for the community. Since the party, I have met so many more lovely people in the area. More than a few have subtly mentioned that there ought to be another party and I haven't ruled out the possibility.

I have been working in the new/old shed for two years, and renovations are still not finished. When we started I believed that we would reach an end point, where things would be finished and work properly. I am learning so much about the trials of taking care of an old building; the moment one thing is finished, another breaks. This is a fact of life both in my studio and the rest of the house. Since moving into the studio I have had an invasion of insulation-eating ants, a mysterious mineral content in the well water which interfered with my dyes, exploding stoves, leaking sinks, frozen pipes, and blown-up water filters. And that's just in two years! When these things happen, I like to imagine how bored I would be if everything worked perfectly all the time. Similarly, the rest of the house has been full of surprises. After the bat family in the attic relocated, we discovered a snake was sneaking into the shop windows to sun itself in the mornings. I was fine with this, but apparently snakes in the house are not welcome. Holes were closed and it has moved on. Woodpeckers are hard at work excavating insects from under the cedar shingles and the basement reliably floods every spring. Getting to know this building, it seems, will be an ongoing process. It is creaky, crotchety, full of surprises and has a personality and mind all of its own. My parents and I are simply along for the ride and trying our best to hold it all together.

Typical Viola workdays are similarly unpredictable, which is a surprise to no one considering that it's me at the helm. I am a champion of double-booking and confused

21

Behind the Scenes at Viola

scheduling, which means that a last-minute surge of activity is often the order of the day. We regularly joke that daily operations would run smoothly if only I had someone shadowing me with a diary and notepad. Not likely! Luckily, I work best under pressure and accomplish lots quite quickly once a deadline is in sight. Understanding and accepting this quality in myself has been an ongoing process and I still find myself surprised by plans to visit a friend's cottage on the same weekend as a shop update when I'm supposed to be flying to England.

The Viola team has always been small. It started with me dreaming and playing around with colours, and my mum Jill jumping in to help with everything from labelling yarn to solving problems. Friends have helped over the years, taking up part-time positions or lending a hand when extra help was needed. I have always found it difficult to explain my dyeing process, and teaching another person that process is even more difficult. Viola began with my colour curiosities, and my dyeing process remains improvisational and experimental to this day. While I have had lots of help with all other aspects of the business, until very recently, the dyeing was all down to me.

The move to Mooresburg was a fresh start

and a chance to upgrade in many ways, but felt like going back to the beginning in other ways. Settling into the new space took time, trial and error, and an understanding of life in the country. I'll never forget the faces of the post office employees when I wandered in for the first time with hundreds of parcels. I was used to a speedy and unflappable Toronto post office, but most certainly 'flapped' these folks. "This is YARN?" they'd ask. "Do you have alpacas then?" was the inevitable next question. They still think I'm mad. The mobile service is so spotty that I always stand on the front porch to make phone calls, waving at passing tractors and buggies. The store was in an internet dead zone, so we had to install a great big tower in order to get online.

Perhaps the biggest and happiest surprise of the move was meeting a person who loves making socks as much as I do. Of all the places in this universe, she lives just down the road! Since Brit joined the Viola team in April 2017, we have been slowly but surely organising, sorting, planning, and editing the process and procedure behind the scenes. Her calm, quiet and thoughtful approach to work is a much-needed counterbalance to my flighty and scattered methods. Somehow, we meet in the middle and accomplish great things. She patiently spends as much time as I do staring into the dyepots, and even reminded me about my driving test when I'd completely forgot about it! It turns out that we share a few of the same dreams for the future as well, and I can't wait to see what happens next.

We are currently a team of three – four if you count Lucy the dog, who is always happy to distract us with a game of chase. Like I say, there is no such thing as a typical Viola work day. The days often feel more like a surprise adventure in creative problem solving than the daily operations of a business, and I believe this is a feeling shared among most small business owners. Our out-of-the-way location provides just enough separation from the bustling world beyond, and our spotty internet is sometimes more of a blessing than a curse. Life and work in Mooresburg are intertwined, and both influenced by the grounding effects of simply watching the seasons pass.

the patterns

My creative process is somewhat scattered, to put it mildly.

I begin with a vague idea, and through swatching, drawing and reading (and often lying awake at night), the fog clears to reveal a picture of what I want to make. Each of these designs began from a different source of inspiration and a specific part of the winter landscape. What helped me to clear the fog, and to steer the design process, was my goal of balancing winter's magic and mystery with the practical necessities of keeping warm. Magic and practicality are somewhat opposing forces, and searching for a balance between them is what fuelled the creation of these patterns.

I often daydream about the lives of the people who settled in Mooresburg in the 1850s. How cold winters must have been for them! Local history books depict almost no knitwear, which is surprising considering that it was largely English, Scottish and Irish people who settled in the area. What did they do with their jumpers? I have come to the conclusion that their knitwear was sensibly tucked away under warmer blanket or beaver coats. Layering is the key to keeping warm, as we all know.

With this in mind, I would like to state that there is nothing at all historically accurate about the patterns in this book. Rather, I have set about making pieces that I think would have been useful to someone trying to survive the harsh winters back then. These people would have needed warm and comfortable clothes that were easy to move and work in, to layer up for extra warmth, or cast aside during a brisk uphill snowshoe. I have read one account of a man called Walter Stoddart walking 18 miles through 2 feet of snow to collect a 100-pound bag (that's 45 kilos!) of flour and carrying it back again in the same day . I know he wanted some comfortable socks for that journey!

These were people whose lives were deeply connected to and reliant on the land, and so I have imagined their wardrobe emerging from the land. It's as if the people and their knitwear are so linked to the winter landscape that they have become a part of it themselves. Of course brushed mohair and silk yarn was nowhere to be seen in Mooresburg 100 years ago, but it's still fun to imagine.

Understated shapes, lines and textures in these designs hint at the more detailed and complex shapes that spend winter buried under layers of snow. Like the quiet subtlety of winter itself, they may not jump out at you straight away. Instead, you may discover these details as you knit, when you select your colours, or finally wear the finished piece.

I have taken inspiration from elements of the winter landscape that I enjoy, and have chosen colours to suit the way I remember a specific day or scene. Winter is an introspective time, and so much of its magic is in our individual perceptions of it. We each experience winter very differently and I hope that these patterns share some of the beauty that I see in its frozen landscape. I also hope that each knitter will add their own winter interpretations to the projects they choose to knit.

A few words about positive ease:
Admittedly, I am a person who prefers to wear positive ease all of the time, but I also believe that it is essential for staying warm. My wise grandpa's advice was to wear lots of roomy layers that would trap little pockets of air around your body, and it's always worked for me. As keeping warm ranks high on a list of practical winter concerns, I've aimed to make each of these designs as warm as possible.

EASTWIND

Eastwind was one of the first designs to take shape. I knew from the start that I wanted to create a substantial warm jacket, because that is exactly what I want every year. Winter winds can be fearsome when whipping across an open field, and as the weightiest garment in this collection, Eastwind is the perfect layer for facing them. Tiny crossed stitches move diagonally across the four body pieces, as if being blown by the wind. They flicker as the jacket moves, and add density and substance to its fabric.

Eastwind Jacket

Sizes: 1 (2, 3, 4)
Finished bust circumference: 115.5 (134.5, 153.5, 172.5) cm / 45½ (53, 60½, 68)" – to be worn with 35.5-50 cm / 14-20" ease
Model has 84 cm / 33" bust, is wearing a size 2, with 50 cm / 20" positive ease.
Yarns: Viola Shadow DK (DK weight; 50% Polwarth, 35% Wensleydale, 15% Zwartbles; 283 m / 308 yds per 100 g skein)
Viola Mohair Lace (lace weight; 72% Mohair, 28% Silk; 420 m / 459 yds per 50 g skein)
Shades:
Yarn A: Shadow DK, Frozen Earth; 4 (5, 6, 7) skeins
Yarn B: Mohair Lace, Bronte; 2 (3, 3, 4) skeins
Yarn C: Shadow DK, Down to the Wire; 1 skein
Gauge: 21 sts & 28 rows = 10 cm / 4" over Body Pattern A or B on 4 mm needles, with 1 strand each of yarns A and B held together, after blocking
10 sts of cable panel = 4.5 cm / 1¾" wide
Needles: 4 mm / US 6 circular needle, 80-100 cm / 32-40" length
AND needles suitable for working small circumferences in the round
3.5 mm / US 4 knitting needles, for working pockets
Note: Although the body of Eastwind is worked flat, a circular needle is recommended to hold the stitches easily.
Always use a needle size that will result in the correct gauge after blocking.
Notions: 2 stitch markers, cable needle, scrap yarn in a contrasting colour, 5-7 toggles or buttons, 5-7 locking stitch markers, tapestry needle
Notes: Eastwind Jacket is knit flat, in pieces, from the bottom up, holding one strand of Shadow DK together with one strand of Mohair Lace. The body is knit in 4 pieces: Front Right & Left and Back Right & Left. Sleeve stitches are cast onto body pieces as they are knit and simple cables line the centre front and back of the garment. Short row shaping adds depth to the back pieces, and shoulders are shaped with Bias Cast Off to form a tidy exposed seam along top of the arms. Seams along the bottom of the arms, centre back and sides are all exposed. Pocket openings are formed while knitting the front pieces, and pockets are worked after the body is seamed. Stitches are picked up in the selvedge edge of sleeves for lower sleeves and are finished in the round, in 1x1 rib to the cuff. Slipped stitches at the beginning of every row ensure a neat selvedge and tidy visible seams on the centre back and sides. Front pieces are smaller in width than back pieces, allowing the garment to hang forwards slightly and hug the wearer. Generous positive ease creates drape and allows for layering up to face cold winter days.

Stitch Glossary
LT: Insert needle into second st on LH needle, knit this st without slipping it off the needle. Knit first st on LH needle and slip both sts off needle.

RT: Slip 2 sts kwise, then slip them back to LH needle putting a twist into the second st (the first st being slipped back onto left-hand needle). Knit into back loop of second st on LH needle (this is the twisted st) without slipping it off the needle, knit first st and slip both sts off the needle.

2/2 RC: Slip 2 sts to cable needle and hold in back, k2, k2 from cable needle
2/2 LC: Slip 2 sts to cable needle and hold in front, k2, k2 from cable needle

Body Pattern A
Used for Left Front and Right Back
(worked over a multiple of 10 sts)
Row 1 (RS): [K1, RT, k7] to end.
Row 2 and all WS rows: Purl.
Row 3: Knit.
Row 5: [K6, RT, k2] to end.
Row 7: Knit.
Row 8 (WS): Purl.
Rep rows 1-8 for pattern.

Body Pattern B
Used for Right Front and Left Back
(worked over a multiple of 10 sts)
Row 1 (RS): [K7, LT, k1] to end.
Row 2 and all WS rows: Purl.
Row 3: Knit.
Row 5: [K2, LT, k6] to end.
Row 7: Knit.
Row 8 (WS): Purl.
Rep rows 1-8 for pattern.

Cable Band A
Used for Left Front and Right Back
(worked over 10 sts)
Row 1 (RS): K1, p1, k1, k4, k1, p1, k1.
Row 2 and all WS rows: K3, p4, k3.
Row 3: K1, p1, k1, 2/2 RC, k1, p1, k1.
Row 5: K1, p1, k1, k4, k1, p1, k1.
Row 6 (WS): K3, p4, k3.
Rep rows 1-6 for pattern.

Cable Band B
Used for Right Front and Left Back
(worked over 10 sts)
Row 1 (RS): K1, p1, k1, k4, k1, p1, k1.
Row 2 and all WS rows: K3, p4, k3.

Eastwind Jacket

Row 3: K1, p1, k1, 2/2 LC, k1, p1, k1.
Row 5: K1, p1, k1, k4, k1, p1, k1.
Row 6: K3, p4, k3.
Rep rows 1-6 for pattern.

Bias Cast Off:
Row 1: Cast off required number of sts as normal.
Row 2: Patt to last st, sl1 pwise.
All foll cast-off rows: Sl2 pwise. Cast off required number of sts, including 2 slipped sts.

Afterthought Button Loop:
You will need a length of working yarn approx. 75 cm / 30" for each button loop, 5 locking stitch markers, and a tapestry needle. If you are using more or fewer toggles / buttons you will need to adjust yarn and markers accordingly.
Mark out button loops using locking stitch markers: Working on WS of band, and 1 row in from cast-off edge, space out markers where button loops are desired.
Form Loops: Using tapestry needle and length of yarn, thread yarn through st above marked st, leaving a tail. Leaving a loop large enough to pass your toggle/button through, thread yarn through st under marked st. Repeat, creating a double stranded loop. Double check that your button loop is the correct size.
Secure the Button Loop by working Blanket Stitch as follows: Thread needle and yarn through double stranded loop from back to front, but do not pull it through all the way. Thread needle from front to back through the little loop just made. Gently tighten and wiggle stitch to the edge of button loop. Repeat blanket stitch until entire button loop has been filled in. When working first and last blanket stitches, stitch into button bands to better secure the button loop. Repeat for remaining button loops.

PATTERN BEGINS

RIGHT FRONT
Using yarn C, larger needles and long-tail method, cast on 52 (62, 72, 82) sts.

Edging
Row 1 (WS): Sl1 wyif, p to last st, k1.
Row 2 (RS): Sl1 wyif, k to end.
Cut yarn C, change to 1 strand each of yarns A and B held together.
Row 3 (WS): Sl1 wyif, k to end.

Establish Pattern
Row 1 (RS): Sl1 wyif, work row 1 of Cable Band B, PM, work row 7 of Body Pattern B 4 (5, 6, 7) times, k1.
Row 2 (WS): Sl1 wyif, work next row of Body Pattern B to marker, SM, work next row of Cable Band B, k1.
Continue straight in patt, working next row of Cable Band B and Body Pattern B each time, until piece measures approximately 15 cm / 6" from cast-on edge, ending with a WS row.

Establish Pocket
Next row (RS): Patt across 13 (18, 23, 28) sts, place locking stitch marker in WS side of next st, patt across 26 sts, place a second locking stitch marker in WS side of next st, patt across 13 (18, 23, 28) sts to end.
Note: Locking stitch markers identify bottom corners of pocket.
Continue straight in patt until piece measures 30.5 cm / 12", ending with a WS row.

Pocket Opening
Cast off Row (RS): Patt 13 (18, 23, 28) sts, cast off next 26 sts, patt to end. *26 (36, 46, 56) sts*
Next Row (WS): Patt 13 (18, 23, 28) sts, using scrap yarn and provisional cast on, cast on 26 sts to LH needle, p26 using working yarns, patt to end. *52 (62, 72, 82) sts*
Continue straight in patt until piece measures 35.5 cm / 14", ending with a WS row.

Armpit Gusset
Stitches are now increased at side seam edge, to create sleeves.
Row 1 (RS): Sl1 wyif, patt to last st, PM, M1L, k1. *1 st inc*
Row 2 (WS): Sl1 wyif, patt to end.
Row 3 (RS): Work as set to second marker, SM, M1L, k to end. *1 st inc*
Rep rows 2-3 a further 5 times, then work row 2 **only** once more. *59 (69, 79, 89) sts*

Cast on for Sleeve
Row 1 (RS): Patt to second marker, SM, k to end.
Row 2 (WS): Using working yarns and cable method, cast on 33 sts to LH needle, p to marker, remove marker, patt to end. *92 (102, 112, 122) sts*
Row 3: Patt to marker, SM, work Body Pattern B 8 (9, 10, 11) times, k1.
Row 4: Patt to end.
Rep rows 3-4 until armhole measures 20 (21.5, 24, 26.5) cm / 8 (8½, 9½, 10½)" from cable cast-on for sleeves, ending with a WS row.

Shape Shoulder
Maintain Cable Band B and Body Pattern B as set.
Row 1 (RS): Patt to end.
Row 2 (WS): Cast off 18 (18, 16, 18) sts, patt to end. *74 (84, 96, 104) sts*
Row 3: Patt to last st, sl1 pwise.
Row 4: Sl2 pwise, cast off 18 (15, 18, 20) sts beg with 2 slipped sts on RH needle, patt to end. *56 (69, 78, 84) sts*
Continuing to work Bias Cast Off method as set, cast off 16 (15, 18,

20) sts at beg of WS rows a further 2 (3, 3, 3) times. *24 sts*

Collar
Row 1 (RS): Sl1 wyif, work Cable Band B, SM, k to end.
Row 2 (WS): Sl1 wyif, p to marker, SM, work Cable Band B, k1.
Rep rows 1-2 until collar measures 4 cm / 1½" ending with a RS row.
With yarn C, knit 2 rows.
Cast off all sts purlwise.

LEFT FRONT
Cast on 52 (62, 72, 82) sts and work edging as for Right Front.

Establish Pattern
Row 1 (RS): Sl1 wyif, work row 7 of Body Pattern A 4 (5, 6, 7) times, PM, work Row 1 of Cable Band A, k1.
Row 2 (WS): Sl1 wyif, work next row of Cable Band A, SM, work next row of Body Pattern A to last st, k1.
Continue straight in patt, working next row of Cable Band A and Body Pattern A each time, until piece measures approximately 15 cm / 6" from cast-on edge, ending with a WS row.

Establish Pockets, and work to Pocket Opening as for Right Front, maintaining Cable Band A and Body Pattern A as set.
Continue straight in patt until piece measures approximately 35.5 cm / 14" from cast-on edge, ending with a WS row.

Armpit Gusset
Row 1 (RS): Sl1 wyif, M1R, PM, work Body Pattern A to marker, SM, work Cable Band A to last st, k1. *1 st inc*
Row 2 (WS): [Patt to marker, SM] twice, p to last st, k1.
Row 3: Sl1 wyif, k to marker, M1R, SM, patt to end. *1 st inc*
Rep rows 2-3 a further 5 times, then work Row 2 **only** once more. *59 (69, 79, 89) sts*

Cast on for Sleeve
Row 1 (RS): Using working yarns and cable method, cast on 33 sts to LH needle, k to marker, SM, patt to end. *92 (102, 112, 122) sts*
Row 2 (WS): Patt to second marker, remove marker, p to last st, k1.
Row 3: Sl1 wyif, work Body Pattern A 8 (9, 10, 11) times, SM, work Cable Band A to last st, k1.
Row 4: Patt to end.
Rep rows 3-4 until armhole measures 20 (21.5, 24, 26.5) cm / 8 (8½, 9½, 10½)" from cable cast-on for sleeves, ending with a row 4.

Shape Shoulder
Maintain Cable Band A and Body pattern A as set.
Row 1 (RS): Cast off 18 (18, 16, 18) sts, patt to end. *74 (84, 96, 104) sts*
Row 2 (WS): Patt to last st, sl1 pwise.
Row 3: Sl2 pwise, cast off 18 (15, 18, 20) sts beg with 2 slipped sts on RH needle, patt to end. *56 (69, 78, 84) sts*
Continuing to work Bias Cast Off method as set, cast off 16 (15, 18, 20) sts at beg of RS rows a further 2 (3, 3, 3) times. *24 sts*
Next row (WS): Patt to last st, k1.

Collar
Row 1 (RS): Sl1 wyif, work Body Pattern A to marker, SM, work Cable Band A to last st, k1.
Row 2 (WS): Patt to end.
Rep rows 1-2 until collar measures 4 cm / 1½", ending with a RS row.
With yarn C, knit 2 rows.
Cast off all sts pwise.

RIGHT BACK
Using yarn C, larger needles and long-tail method, cast on 62 (72, 82, 92) sts.
Work edging as for Right Front.

Establish Pattern
Row 1 (RS): Sl1 wyif, work row 7 of Body Pattern A 5 (6, 7, 8) times, PM, work Row 1 of Cable Band A, k1.
Row 2 (WS): Sl1 wyif, work next row of Cable Band A, SM, work next row of Body Pattern A to last st, k1.
Continue straight in patt, working next row of Cable Band A and Body Pattern A each time, until work measures approx. 35.5 cm / 14" from cast-on edge, ending with a WS row.

Armpit Gusset
Row 1 (RS): Sl1 wyif, M1R, PM, work Body Pattern A to marker, SM, work Cable Band A to last st, k1. *1 st inc*
Row 2 (WS): [Patt to marker, SM] twice, p to last st, k1.
Row 3: Sl1 wyif, k to marker, M1R, SM, patt to end. *1 st inc*
Rep rows 2-3 a further 5 times, then work row 2 **only** once more. *69 (79, 89, 99) sts*

Cast on for Sleeve
Row 1 (RS): Using working yarns and cable method, cast on 33 sts onto LH needle, k to marker, SM, patt to end. *102 (112, 122, 132) sts*
Row 2 (WS): Patt to second marker, remove marker, p to last st, k1.
Row 3: Sl1 wyif, work Body Pattern A to marker, SM, work Cable Band A to last st, k1.
Row 4: Patt to end.
Rep rows 3-4 until armhole measures 20 (21.5, 24, 26.5) cm / 8 (8½, 9½, 10½)" from cable cast-on for sleeves, ending with a WS row.

Shape Back Neck
Row 1 (RS): Sl1 wyif, patt to marker, SM, work Cable Band A to last st, k1.
Row 2 (WS): Sl1 wyif, work Cable Band A to marker, SM, work patt to last

Eastwind Jacket

14 sts, w&t.
Row 3: Rep row 1.
Row 4: Patt to 11 sts before previous w&t, w&t.
Rep rows 3-4 a further 3 times, PM after last w&t. *5 wrapped sts*
Rep row 3 **only** once more.
Next row (WS): Patt to end, concealing wraps and slipping markers as you pass them.

Cast off for Shoulders
Row 1 (RS): Cast off 16 (18, 20, 22) sts, patt to end. *86 (94, 102, 110) sts*
Row 2 (WS): Patt to last st, sl1 pwise.
Row 3 (RS): Sl2 pwise, cast off 13 (15, 17, 19) sts beg with 2 slipped sts on RH needle, patt to end. *73 (79, 85, 91) sts*
Continuing to work Bias Cast Off method as set, cast off 13 (15, 17, 19) sts at beg of RS rows a further 3 times. *34 sts*
Next row (WS): Patt to last st, k1.

Right Back Collar
Row 1 (RS): Sl1 wyif, work Body Pattern A to marker, SM, work Cable Band A to last st, k1.
Row 2 (WS): Patt to end.
Rep rows 1-2 until collar measures 4 cm / 1½", ending with a RS row.
With yarn C, knit 2 rows. Cast off all sts purlwise.

LEFT BACK
Using yarn C, larger needles and long-tail method, cast on 62 (72, 82, 92) sts.
Work edging as for Right Front.

Establish Pattern
Row 1 (RS): Sl1 wyif, work row 1 of Cable Band B, PM, work row 7 of Body Pattern B 5 (6, 7, 8) times, k1.
Row 2 (WS): Sl1 wyif, work next row of Body Pattern B to marker, SM, work next row of Cable Band B, k1.
Continue straight in pattern, working the next row of Cable Band B and Body Pattern B each time, until work measures approx. 35.5 cm / 14" from cast-on edge, ending with a WS row.

Armpit Gusset
Row 1 (RS): Sl1 wyif, M1R, PM, work Body Pattern B to marker, SM, work Cable Band B to last st, k1. *1 st inc*
Row 2 (WS): [Patt to marker, SM] twice, p to last st, k1.
Row 3: Sl1 wyif, k to marker, M1R, SM, patt to end. *1 st inc*
Rep rows 2-3 a further 5 times, then work row 2 **only** once more. *69 (79, 89, 99) sts*

Cast on for Sleeve
Row 1 (RS): [Patt to marker, SM] twice, k to end.
Row 2 (WS): Using working yarns and cable method, cast on 33 sts to LH needle, p to marker, remove marker, patt to end. *102 (112, 122, 132) sts*
Row 3: Patt to marker, SM, work Body Pattern B to last st, k1.
Row 4: Patt to end.
Rep rows 3-4 until armhole measures 20 (21.5, 24, 26.5) cm / 8 (8½, 9½, 10½)" from cable cast-on for sleeves, ending with a row 4.

Shape Back Neck
Row 1 (RS): Patt to last 14 sts, w&t.
Row 2 (WS): Patt to end.
Row 3: Patt to 11 sts before previous w&t, w&t.
Rep rows 2-3 a further 3 times, PM after final w&t. *5 wrapped sts*
Rep row 2 **only** once more.
Row 19 (RS): Patt to end, concealing wraps and slipping markers as you pass them.

Shape Shoulders
Row 1 (WS): Cast off 16 (18, 20, 22) sts, patt to end. *86 (94, 102, 110) sts*
Row 2 (RS): Patt to last st, sl1 pwise.
Row 3 (WS): Sl2 pwise, cast off 13 (15, 17, 19) sts beg with 2 slipped sts on RH needle, patt to end. *73 (79, 85, 91) sts*
Continuing to work Bias Cast Off method as set, cast off 13 (15, 17, 19) sts at beg of WS rows a further 3 times. *34 sts*

Left Back Collar
Row 1 (RS): Sl1 wyif, work Cable Band B, SM, k to end.
Row 2 (WS): Sl1 wyif, p to marker, SM, work Cable Band B, k1.
Rep rows 1-2 until collar measures 4 cm / 1½" ending with a RS row.
With yarn C, knit 2 rows.
Cast off all sts purlwise.

FINISHING
Block Front and Back pieces.
Working on WS to create an exposed seam, and using yarn A, sew shoulder seams, side seams and centre seam at back.

Lower Sleeves
Using yarns A and B held together, larger needles suitable for working small circumferences in the round, and beg at underarm with RS facing, pick up and knit 56 (62, 70, 80) sts around Right Sleeve opening. Join for working in the round. PM to indicate beg of round.
Round 1: [K1, p1] to end.
Rep round 1 for approximately 15 cm / 6" or until desired sleeve length is reached.
Cast off all sts in pattern loosely.
Rep for second sleeve.

Pockets
Using yarn C, and smaller needles, pick up 26 sts between locking stitch markers on the WS of Front piece. Pick up 1 st by inserting your needle into the bottom of a 'frowning' purl bump on the WS of work. It is important to ensure you are picking up sts on a row with no cables as they will make it difficult to pick up in a straight line, so adjust one row up or down if marked row was a cable row.
Turn work.

Work in St st, beg with a knit row, until inside pocket measures approximately 15 cm / 6". Work should be in line with bound off sts for pocket opening.
Carefully unravel provisional cast-on and pick up 26 live sts along upper edge of pocket. Using yarn C, graft 26 held pocket sts to 26 live pocket sts.
Rep for second pocket.

Right Button Band
Using yarns A and B held together, larger needles, and beg at hem edge of Right Front with RS facing, pick up and knit approx. 88 (92, 94, 98) sts in slipped stitch selvedge.
Work 7 rows in St st, beg with a purl (WS) row. Cast off all sts.

Make button loops using Afterthought Button Loop technique, evenly distributing them as desired along Right Button Band.

Afterthought button Loops will take up about 3 sts in width, so bear this in mind when distributing. Sample spaces out button loops every 12-14 sts (e.g. 11 sts between each loop).

Left Button Band
Using yarns A and B held together, larger needles, and beg at neck edge of Left Front with RS facing, pick up and knit approx. 88 (92, 94, 98) sts in slipped stitch selvedge.

Work 17 rows in St st, beg with a purl (WS) row. Cast off all sts.

Sew down side of pockets on WS of work using yarn A, and mattress stitch. Insert tapestry needle into 'frowning' purl sts from the bottom up when sewing down pockets to ensure seam is almost entirely invisible from RS of work.
Attach toggles or buttons to centre of Left Button Bands.
Weave in all ends and block to measurements.

A. Bust circumference: 115.5 (134.5, 153.5, 172.5) cm / 45½ (53, 60½, 68)"
B: Total length: 55.5 (57, 59.5, 62) cm / 22 (22½, 23½, 24½)"
C: Front piece width at hem: 25.5 (30, 35, 39.5) cm / 10 (11¾, 13¾, 15½)"
D: Back piece width at hem: 30 (35, 39.5, 44.5) cm / 11¾ (13¾, 15½, 17½)"
E: Back neck width: 30 cm / 12"
F: Armhole depth: 20 (21.5, 24, 26.5) cm / 8 (8½, 9½, 10½)"
G: Body to underarm length: 35.5 cm / 14"
H: Shoulder/Sleeve width: 44.5 (49.5, 54, 59) cm / 17½ (19½, 21¼, 23¼)"
I: Lower sleeve circumference: 27.5 (29.5, 34, 38) cm / 10¾ (11¾, 13½, 15)"
J: Lower sleeve length: 15 cm / 6"

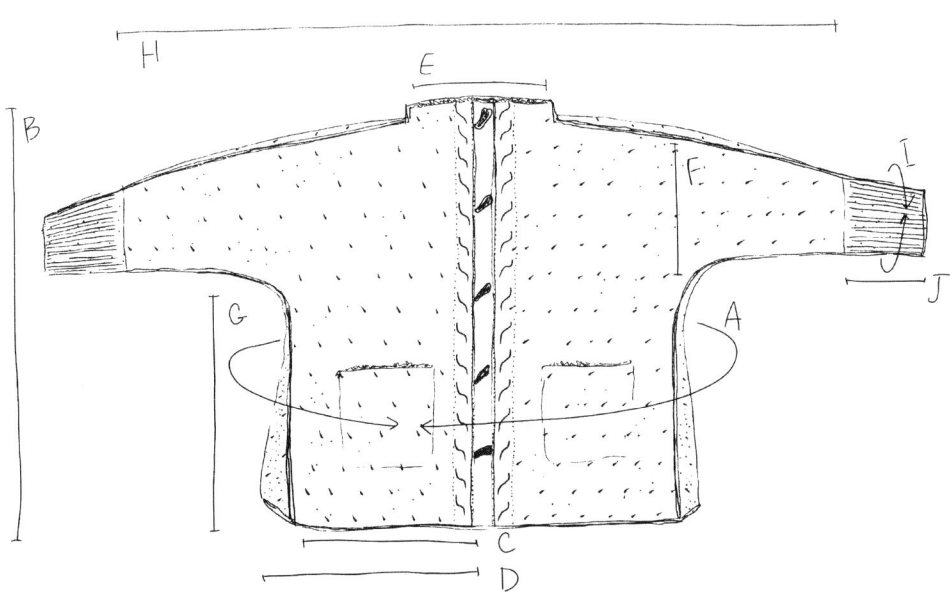

Snowdrift

As you may well imagine, I spent a lot of time staring at snow while working on these patterns. I love how it softens out the sharp edges of the objects beneath it, creating smooth and undulating lines. I also love that snow's whiteness is a mirror for the many colours of the sky and land, making it anything but white. In Snowdrift, I combined just a few of the colours I have seen in snow. Using random and improvised stripes, I added colour when and where I wanted. I knit the entire shawl holding one strand of Polwarth & Alpaca together with one strand of Mohair Lace, a favourite yarn pairing that is also used in the original Soirée sweater (pg 86). To create the stripes, I incorporated an additional strand of mohair lace in one of my contrasting colours. No stripe is more than five rows deep, and I always knit my stripes over an odd number of rows, leaving a colourful tail at the beginning and end of the row. I knit the tails into the shawl body, rather than sewing their ends in after the knitting was finished.

There were two reasons for my use of improvised stripes, tiny amounts of many colours, and carefree tidying of ends. First, I know that the folks of Mooresburg 100 years ago would probably have used up every last scrap of yarn they had. Today we have an incredible selection of beautiful yarn to knit with, yet I think there is still value and satisfaction to be found in using what we have and not wasting. I chose little bits of mohair that I had lying around for this sample (luckily I had lots of 'snow reflection' colours). My second reason for this haphazard approach was to mimic the movement of the snow, light and colours that are constantly changing outside the window. These things are not uniform and patterned, and neither are the stripes of this shawl.

39

Snowdrift Shawl

One Size: 102 cm / 40" wingspan, 80 cm / 32" depth from centre back to point
Yarn A: Viola Polwarth + Alpaca (4 ply / Fingering weight; 70% Polwarth, 15% Brown Alpaca, 15% White Alpaca; 500 m / 547 yds per 100 g skein)
Shade: Silver Birch; 3 skeins
Yarn B: Viola Mohair Lace (lace weight; 72% Mohair, 28% Silk; 420 m / 459 yds per 50 g skein)
Shades:
MC: Cygnet; 3 skeins
CC 1-7: Ghost, Dew Drop, Bronte, Frozen Earth, Down to the Wire, Evergreen, Giant Peach; approx. 10 g each.
Note: Borders take approx. 25 g of yarn B. If you plan to stripe borders as well, more of yarn B will be required.
Note on Yarn B CC: Only tiny amounts of each colour are used so this is a great opportunity to use up any little bits of leftover yarn in your own stash. A fluffy mohair blends in well, but choose contrasting stripes in colours that work well together, and you will enjoy wearing. This shawl is about using what you have, not having to hunt down 7 matching colours. I'd recommend a few colour swatches, and taking the time to experiment with colour combinations and placement before casting on. It's an opportunity to dig out some treasures from your stash!
Gauge: 10 cm / 4" over Brioche Garter stitch on 4 mm needles, with 1 strand each of yarns A and B held together, after blocking
15 sts & 42 rows = 10 cm / 4" over Garter stitch on 4.5 mm needles after blocking
Needles: 4 mm / US 6 circular needle, 100 cm / 40" length
4.5 mm / US 7 circular needle, 80-100 cm / 32-40" length for borders
Note: Although the shawl is worked flat, a circular needle is recommended due to the large number of sts.
Always use a needle size that will result in the correct gauge after blocking.
Notions: 2 stitch markers, tapestry needle
Notes: Snowdrift Shawl is an 'almost triangular' shawl. It is cast on at the lower tip and yarnover increases are worked at the beginning and end of RS rows until the shawl reaches its widest point. Brioche lines run vertically up and down the shawl body, and repeats are incorporated into the body as increases are worked. Stitches for the border are picked up in the yarnover increases of the shawl body. Short rows are used to shape the borders, and border stitches are knit on a larger needle to prevent the shawl body from puckering.
The body is knit holding one strand of yarn A and one strand of yarn B MC together throughout. Contrasting stripes are knit in yarn B CC, and make up a third strand in areas where they are used. The pictured shawl uses seven contrasting yarn B colours at random to create the stripe pattern. The border is knit with one strand of yarn A and one strand of yarn B CC held double. Stripes of yarn B CC can also be worked at the border if preferred.
At the beg and end of Row 1 of the Brioche Garter pattern there is a double yo (a yo and a sl1yo next to each other). Remember to work both yarn overs. When working back across the WS on the foll row, work the first double yo as [k1, brp] and the second double yo as [brp, k1].

Stitch Glossary
Brioche Garter (multiple of 7 sts)
Row 1 (RS): [Sl1yo, k6] to end.
Row 2 (WS): [K6, brp] to end.
Rep rows 1-2 for pattern.

PATTERN BEGINS
Set-up
Using smaller needles, yarns A and B held together and the long-tail method, cast on 3 sts.

Refer to Snowdrift Set-up Chart, or follow written instructions below, striping yarn B CC randomly throughout (see Pattern Notes):
Row 1 (RS): [K1, yo] twice, k1. *5 sts*
Row 2 (WS): K2, p1, k2.
Row 3: K1, yo, k1, sl1yo, k1, yo, k1. *7 sts*
Row 4: K3, brp, k3.
Row 5: K1, yo, k2, sl1yo, k2, yo, k1. *9 sts*
Row 6: K4, brp, k4.
Row 7: K1, yo, k3, sl1yo, k3, yo, k1. *11 sts*
Row 8: K5, brp, k5.
Row 9: K1, yo, k4, sl1yo, k4, yo, k1. *13 sts*
Row 10: K6, brp, k6.
Row 11: K1, yo, k5, sl1yo, k5, yo, k1. *15 sts*
Row 12: K7, brp, k7.
Row 13: K1, yo, k6, sl1yo, k6, yo, k1. *17 sts*
Row 14: K1, p1, k6, brp, k6, p1, k1.

Brioche Garter Body
Refer to Brioche Garter Chart for remainder of Body (note that markers are not shown on the chart), or follow written instructions below, continuing to stripe yarn B CC throughout:
Row 1 (RS): K1, yo, PM, [sl1yo, k6] to last 2 sts, sl1yo, PM, yo, k1. *2 sts inc*
Row 2 (WS): K2, SM, [brp, k6] to last 3 sts, brp, SM, k2.
Row 3: K1, yo, k to marker, SM, [sl1yo, k6] to 1 st before marker, sl1yo, SM, k to last st, yo, k1. *2 sts inc*
Row 4: K to marker, SM, [brp, k6] to 1 st before marker, brp, SM, k to end.

Snowdrift Shawl

Rows 5-13: Rep rows 3-4 a further 4 times, then rep row 3 **only** once more, removing markers. *10 sts inc*
Row 14 (WS): K1, p1, k6, [brp, k6] to last 2 sts, p1, k1.
Rep rows 1-14 a further 19 times. *297 sts*
Rep rows 1-4 once more. *301 sts*
Cast off all sts loosely.

Left Border
With RS facing, using larger needles and yarns A and B MC held together, pick up and knit 149 sts from point B to point C (refer to schematic), picking up 1 st in each yo.
Knit 2 rows.

Begin Short Row shaping:
Next row (RS): K to last 4 sts, turn work.
Next row (WS): Knit.
Repeat previous 2 rows until a total of 27 garter ridges (54 rows) have been worked at the widest part of border, ending with a WS Row.
Knit 2 rows across all sts.
Cast off all sts loosely.

Right Border
With RS facing, using larger needles and yarns A and B MC held together, pick up and knit 149 sts from point A to point B (refer to schematic), picking up 1 st in each yo.
Knit 2 rows.
Next row (RS): Knit.
Next row (WS): K to last 4 sts, turn work.
Complete as for Left Border.

FINISHING
Weave in ends and block to measurements.

A. Wingspan: 102 cm / 40"
B. Depth (centre back to point): 80 cm / 32"

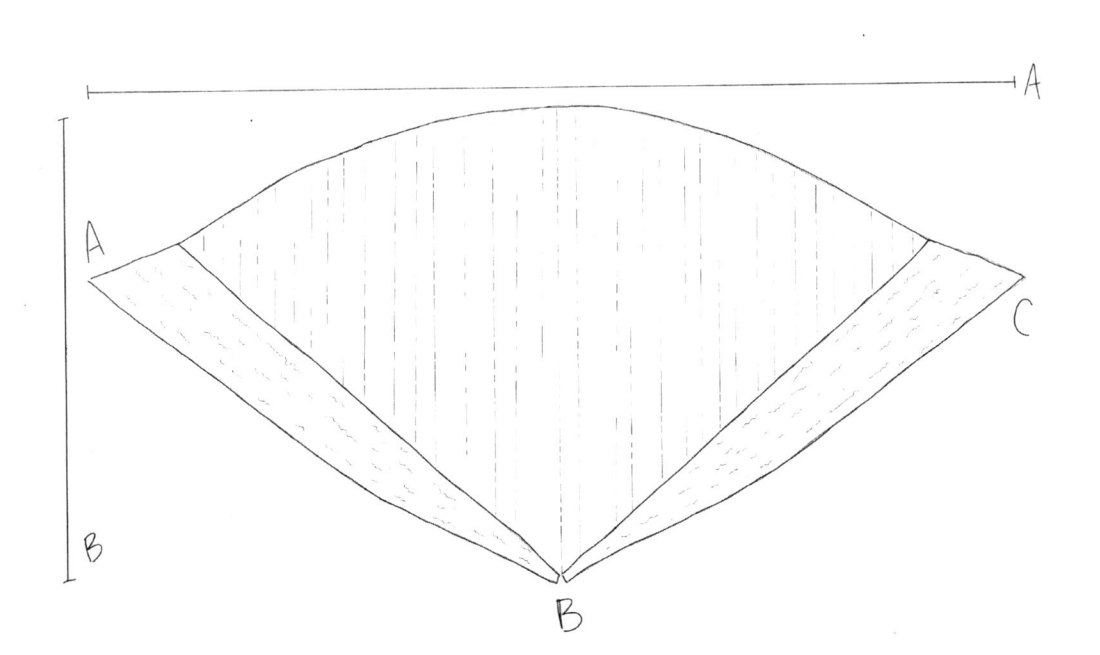

Brioche Garter Chart

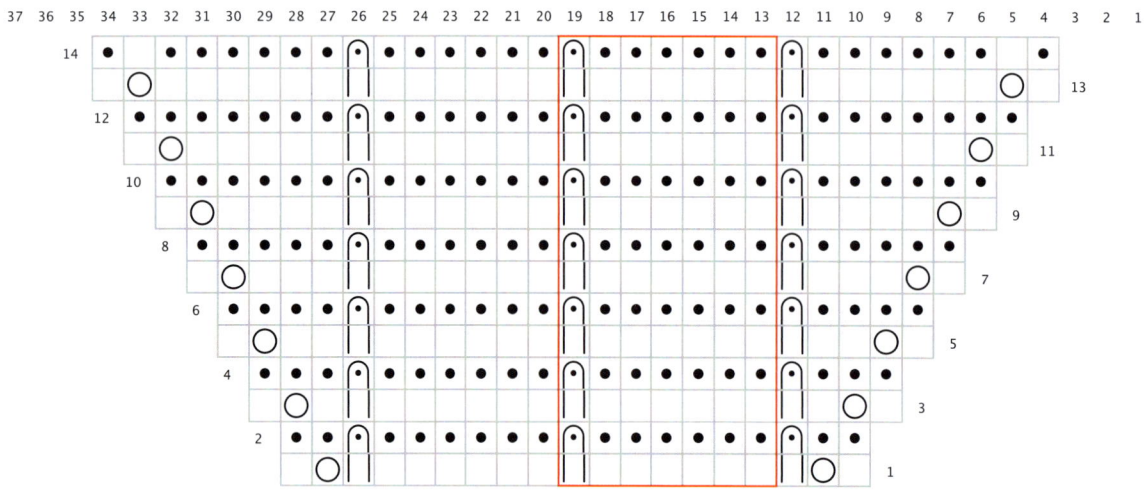

Key
- ☐ RS: knit / WS: purl
- ● RS: purl / WS: knit
- ○ yo
- | sl1yo
- brp
- ▢ Repeat

Set-up Chart

Key
- ☐ RS: knit / WS: purl
- ● RS: purl / WS: knit
- ○ yo
- | sl1yo
- brp

43

Snowshoe Socks are the heavyweight big sister to Favourite Socks (pg 112). They're constructed in much the same way, from two strands of 4-ply yarn held together. I chose to use one strand of durable Sock with one strand of soft and bouncy Merino Fingering, creating a warm, squishy and hardworking sock. Holding two strands together provides an exciting opportunity for colour mixing and pairing, made even more fun when the time comes to think about stripes. I chose to create stripes by breaking just one strand (either Sock or Merino Fingering) while maintaining the other throughout the stripe, blending the stripe into the sock. As always, the colour options are endless. These socks knit up so quickly that you might not be able to stop at just one pair!

Snowshoe

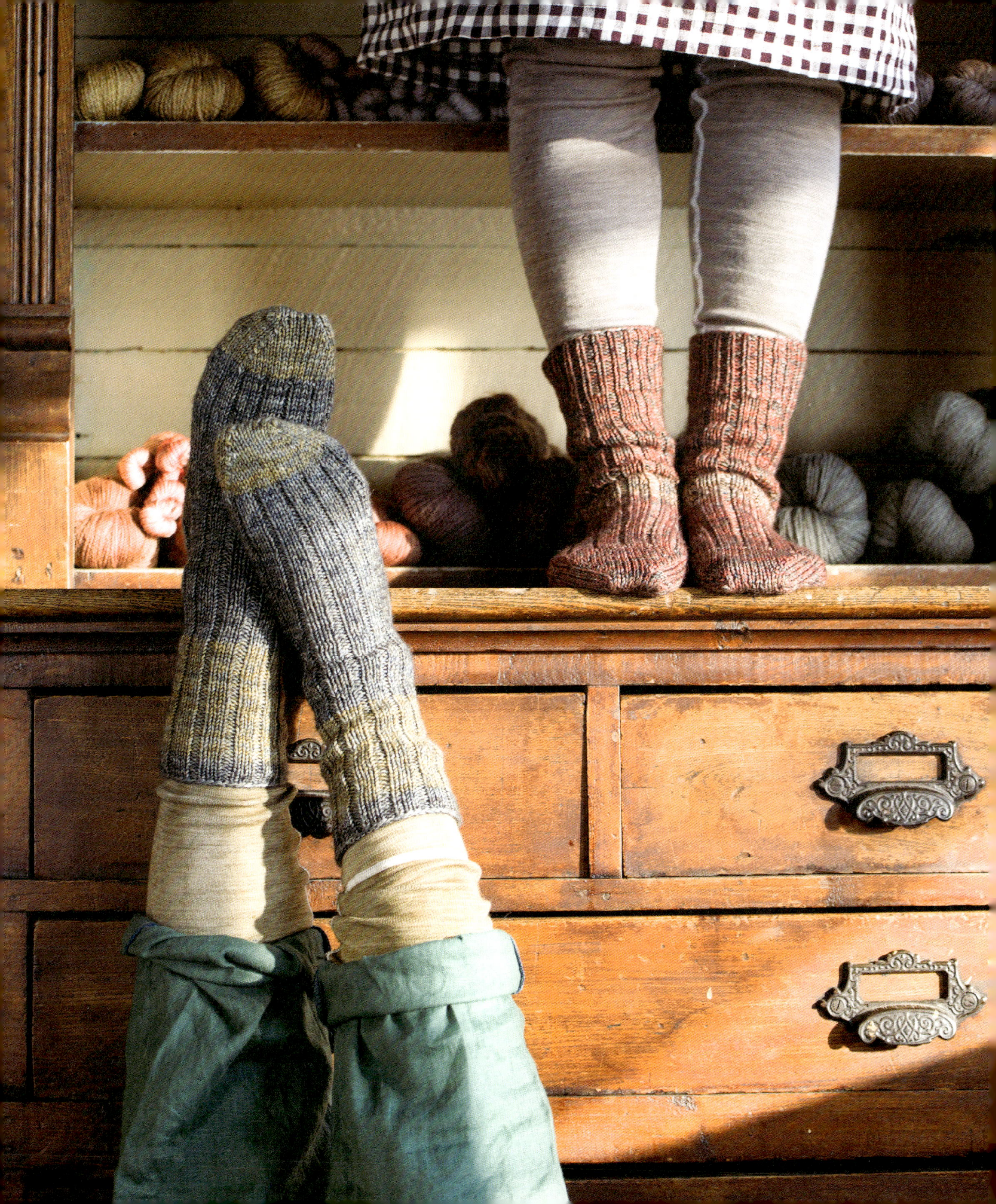

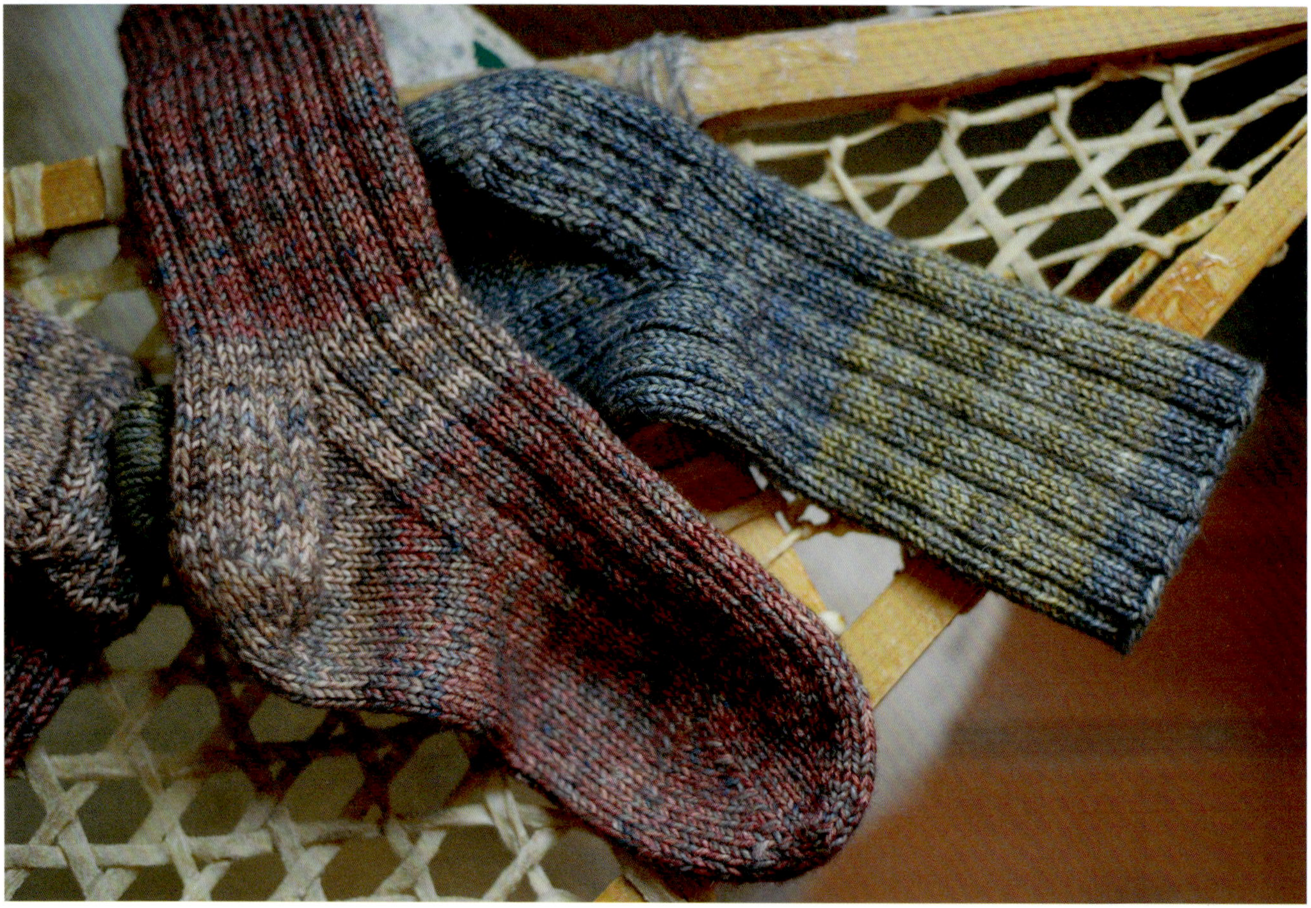

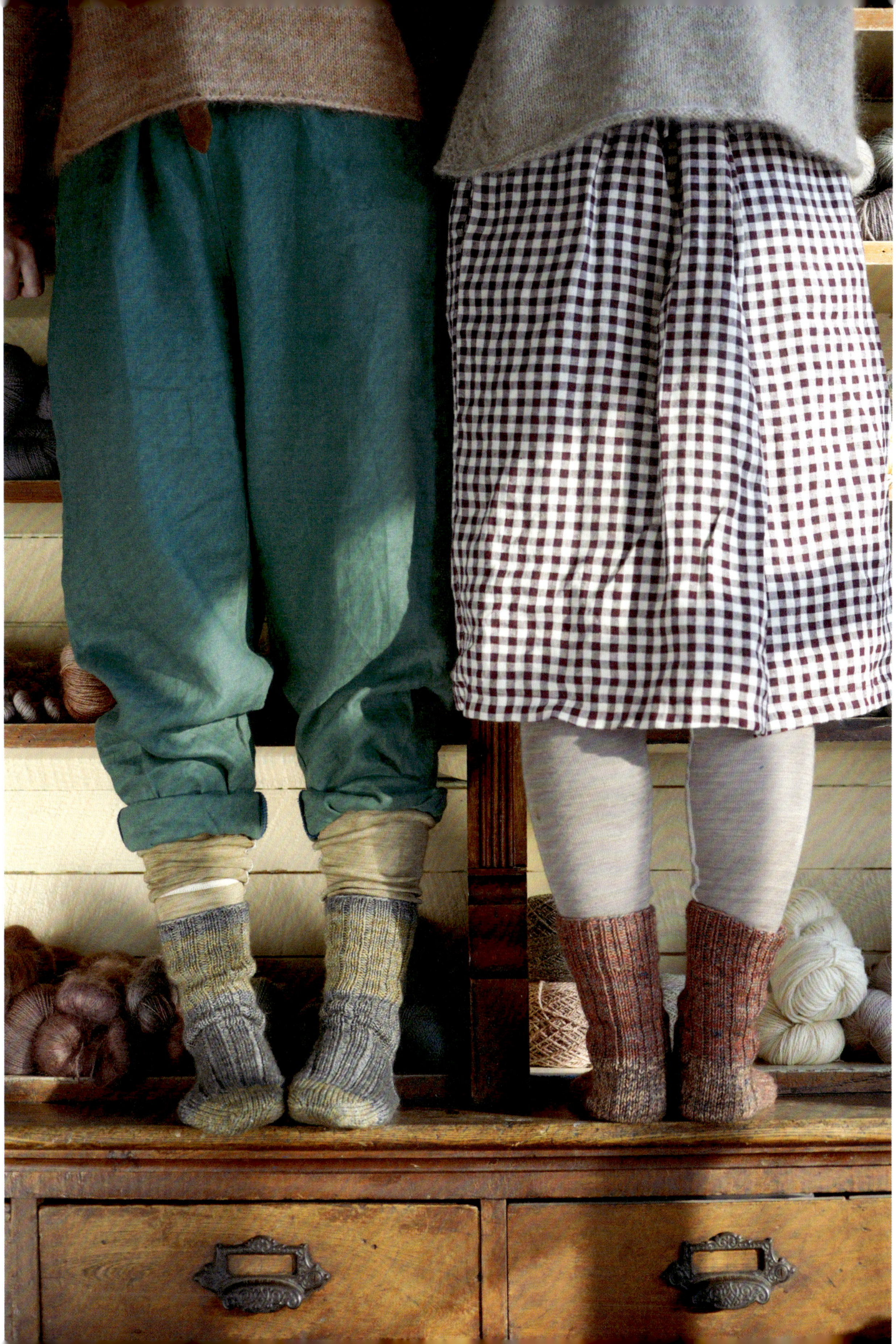

Snowshoe Socks

Sizes: 1 (2, 3)
Finished foot circumference: 18 (21, 24.5) cm / 7 (8¼, 9½)"
Models both wear size 1.
Yarn A: Viola Merino Fingering (4 ply / Fingering weight; 100% Superwash Merino; 366 m / 418 yds per 100 g skein)
Yarn B: Viola Sock (4 ply / Fingering weight; 75% Superwash Merino, 25% Nylon; 421 m / 460 yds per 100 g skein)
Note: For a pair, you will need a total of approximately 120 (130, 140) g or about 480 (520, 560) m / 525 (570, 615) yds of 4 ply / Fingering weight yarn.
Shades:
RED SOCKS
Yarn A: Frozen Earth; 230 (250, 270) m / 250 (275, 295) yds
Yarn B MC: Fireside; 210 (228, 246) m / 230 (250, 270) yds
Yarn B CC: Giant Peach; 42 (46, 50) m / 46 (50, 55) yds
BLUE SOCKS
Yarn A: Midnight; 192 (210, 228) m / 210 (230, 250) yds
Yarn B MC: Evergreen; 170 (182, 201) m / 185 (200, 220) yds
Yarn B CC: Mineral; 86 (92, 100) m / 95 (100, 110) yds
Gauge: 25 sts & 32 rounds = 10 cm / 4" over Body Rib pattern on 3.5 mm needles, with 1 strand each of yarns A and B held together, after blocking
Needles: 3.5 mm / US 4 knitting needles suitable for working small circumferences in the round
Always use a needle size that will result in the correct gauge after blocking.
Notions: Stitch marker, tapestry needle
Notes: Snowshoe socks are knit from the top down, with a heel flap and gusset construction. Yarns A and B are held together throughout, and stripes are included by changing out shades of either yarn A or B.
Notes are included in pattern for sample stripes, but stripe and colour possibilities are endless. Please don't feel limited to the stripes used here!

Stitch Glossary
1x1 Rib (multiple of 2 sts)
Round 1: [K1, p1] to end.
Rep round 1 for pattern.

Body Rib (multiple of 4 sts)
Round 1: [K3, p1] to end.
Rep round 1 for pattern.

Colour Notes
Red pair: When Leg measures 15.5 cm / 6¼", change yarn B to CC and work 4 more rounds of Leg, heel flap, heel turn, and first 7 rounds of gusset shaping. Change yarn B back to MC and work to end.
Blue pair: Work first 6 rounds of leg in yarn A MC and yarn B MC. Change to yarn B CC and work 32 rounds (9.5 cm / 3¾"). Change yarn B back to MC and work to beginning of toe. Work Toe with yarn A MC and yarn B CC.

PATTERN BEGINS
Holding 1 strand each of yarn A MC and yarn B MC together and using the long-tail method, cast on 44 (52, 60) sts. Join for working in the round, being careful not to twist sts. PM to indicate beg of round.

Cuff (optional, shown in Red)
Work 1x1 Rib for 6 cm / 2½" or desired cuff length.

Leg
Work Body Rib for 16 cm / 6½" from cast-on edge or desired leg length.

Arrange sts for heel flap
Next row (RS): Patt over first 21 (25, 29) sts. Turn.
These sts will now be worked in rows to form heel flap. Rearrange rem 23 (27, 31) instep sts so that they are separate from heel sts just worked. Turn work so WS of heel flap is facing.

Heel Flap
Set-up row (WS): Sl1, p to last st, cast on 1 st using backward loop method, p1. *22 (26, 30) sts for heel flap*
Row 1 (RS): [Sl1, k1] to end.
Row 2 (WS): Purl.
Rep rows 1-2 a further 11 (13, 15) times, ending with a row 2.

Heel Turn
Set-up row 1 (RS): K15 (17, 19), ssk, k1, turn.
Set-up row 2 (WS): Sl1, p9, p2tog, p1, turn.
Heel Turn row 1 (RS): Sl1, k to 1 st before gap, ssk, k1, turn.
Heel Turn row 2 (WS): Sl1, p to 1 st before gap, p2tog, p1, turn.
Repeat Heel Turn rows 1-2 until all sts outside of gaps have been decreased, ending with a row 2. *16 (18, 20) sts rem on heel*

Gusset
Next round: Knit across 8 (9, 10) heel sts, PM for new beg of round, knit 8 (9, 10) heel sts, pick up and knit 12 (14, 16) sts in right side heel flap, PM, patt across instep sts, PM, pick up and knit 12 (14, 16) sts in left side heel flap, knit to end of round. *63 (73, 83) sts*

Next round: K8 (9, 10), ktbl to marker, SM, patt across instep sts, SM, ktbl to last 8 (9, 10) sts, k to end.

Decrease for Gusset
Round 1 (Dec): K to 4 sts before marker, k2tog, k2, SM, patt to marker, SM, k2, ssk, k to end. *2 sts dec*
Round 2: Patt to end.
Rep rounds 1-2 a further 7 (8, 9) times, then rep round 1 **only** once more. *45 (53, 61) sts*

Final Decrease Round: K to 4 sts before marker, k2tog, k2, SM, patt to end. *44 (52, 60) sts*

Continue in pattern as set, working instep sts in Body Rib and foot in St st, until foot measures 5 cm / 2½" short of desired length from heel to tip of toe.

Shape Toe
Round 1 (Dec): [K to 4 sts before marker, k2tog, k2, SM, k2, ssk, SM] twice, k to end. *4 sts dec*
Round 2: Knit.
Rep rounds 1-2 until 16 sts rem, then work round 1 **only** once more. *12 sts*
Break yarn, leaving a tail long enough for grafting toe.

FINISHING
Graft toe sts using Kitchener stitch.
Weave in ends and block to measurements.

A. Finished foot circumference: 18 (21, 24.5) cm / 7 (8¼, 9½)"
B. Leg length: 16 cm / 6½"

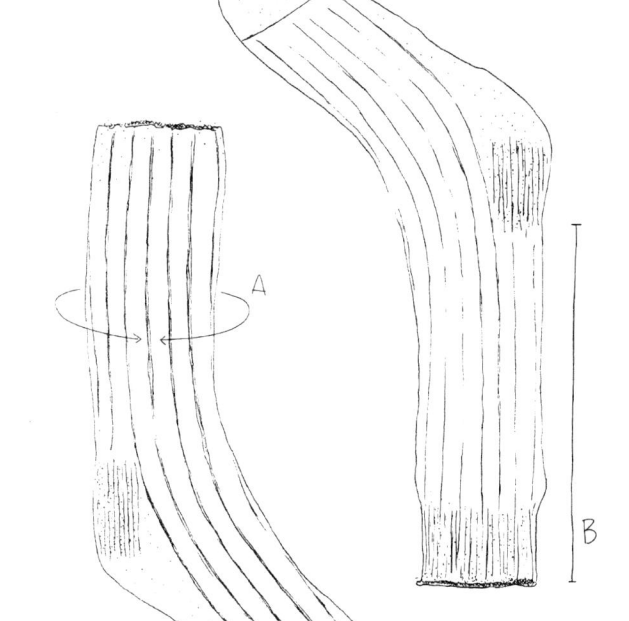

skyhill

For a long time I have searched for a knitted hat and mittens that are thick and warm enough for really, really cold days. Knitted fabric is cosy without doubt, but cold wind blows straight through it. Felting stops the wind, as does layering, but my goal was to make the Skyhill Hat and Mitts thick and warm enough to stop some of that wind. I believe I've succeeded!

Double-stranded DK weight yarn is thick and squishy, and knits up fast. Slipped stitches on the right and wrong sides add extra thickness as well as the coveted warm pocket of air against the skin, based on my grandpa's torture-tested theory. If you don't believe me, just give them a try.

This hat and mitten set didn't find its name until the week that we gathered together in Mooresburg for the book photoshoot. To my delight everyone loved the hat so much that three more were knit within the week, and a fourth finished shortly after. After all our work was finished we ventured out to visit friends at their rather magical home called Skyhill, all wearing our new hats as we walked through the woods. At last, the hat had a name.

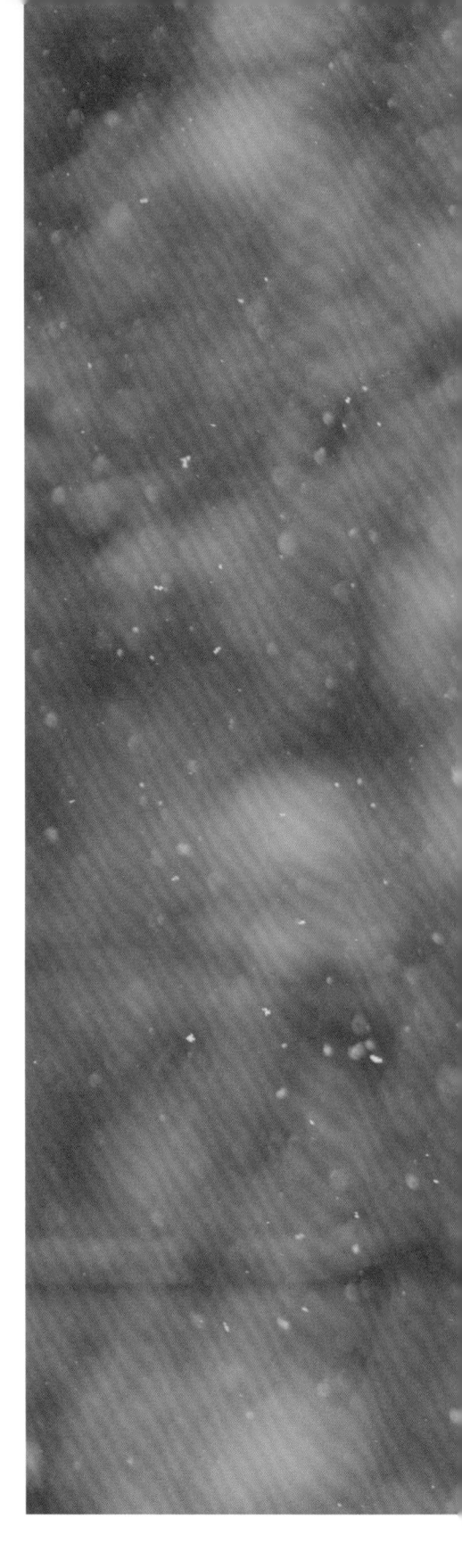

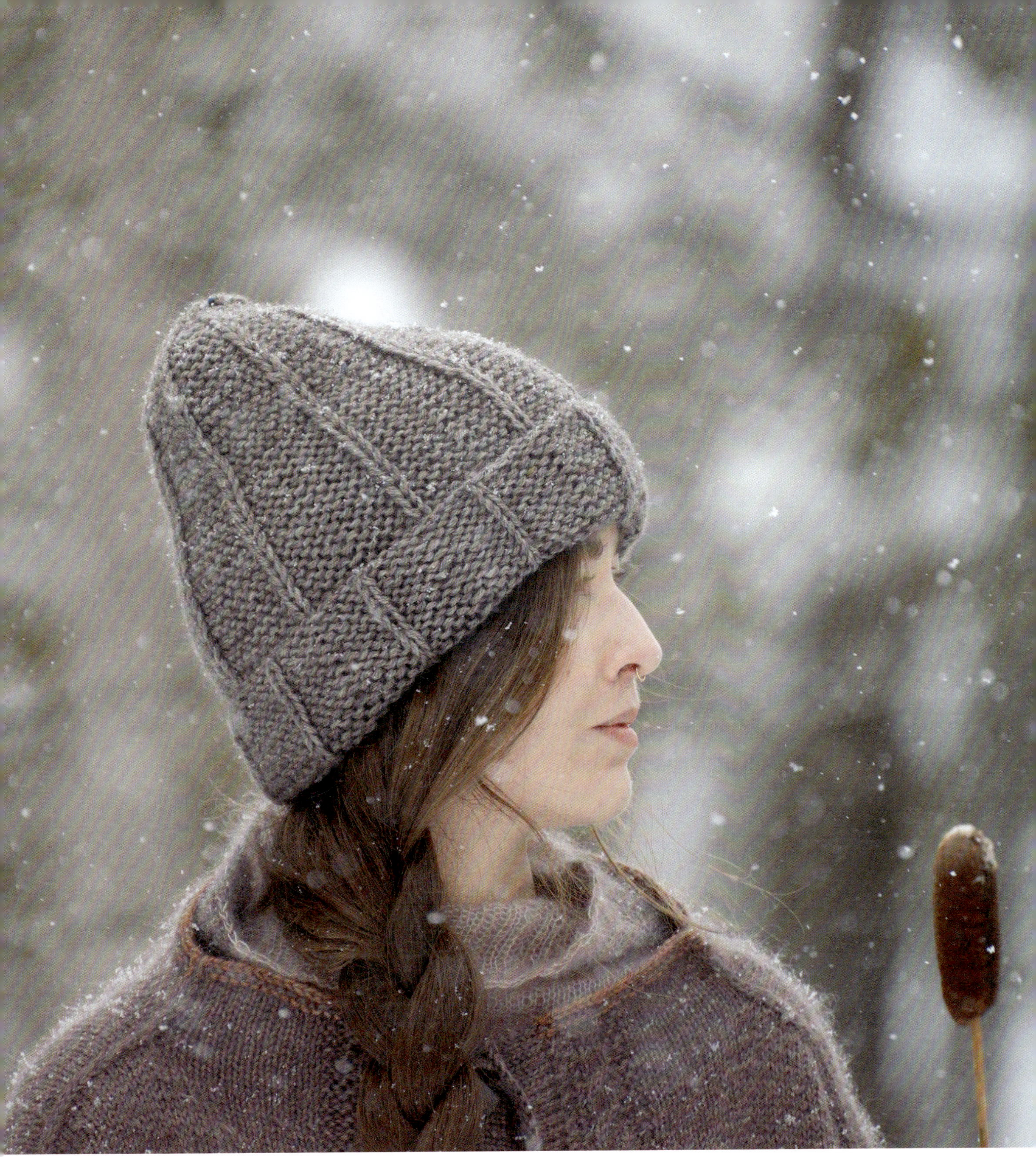

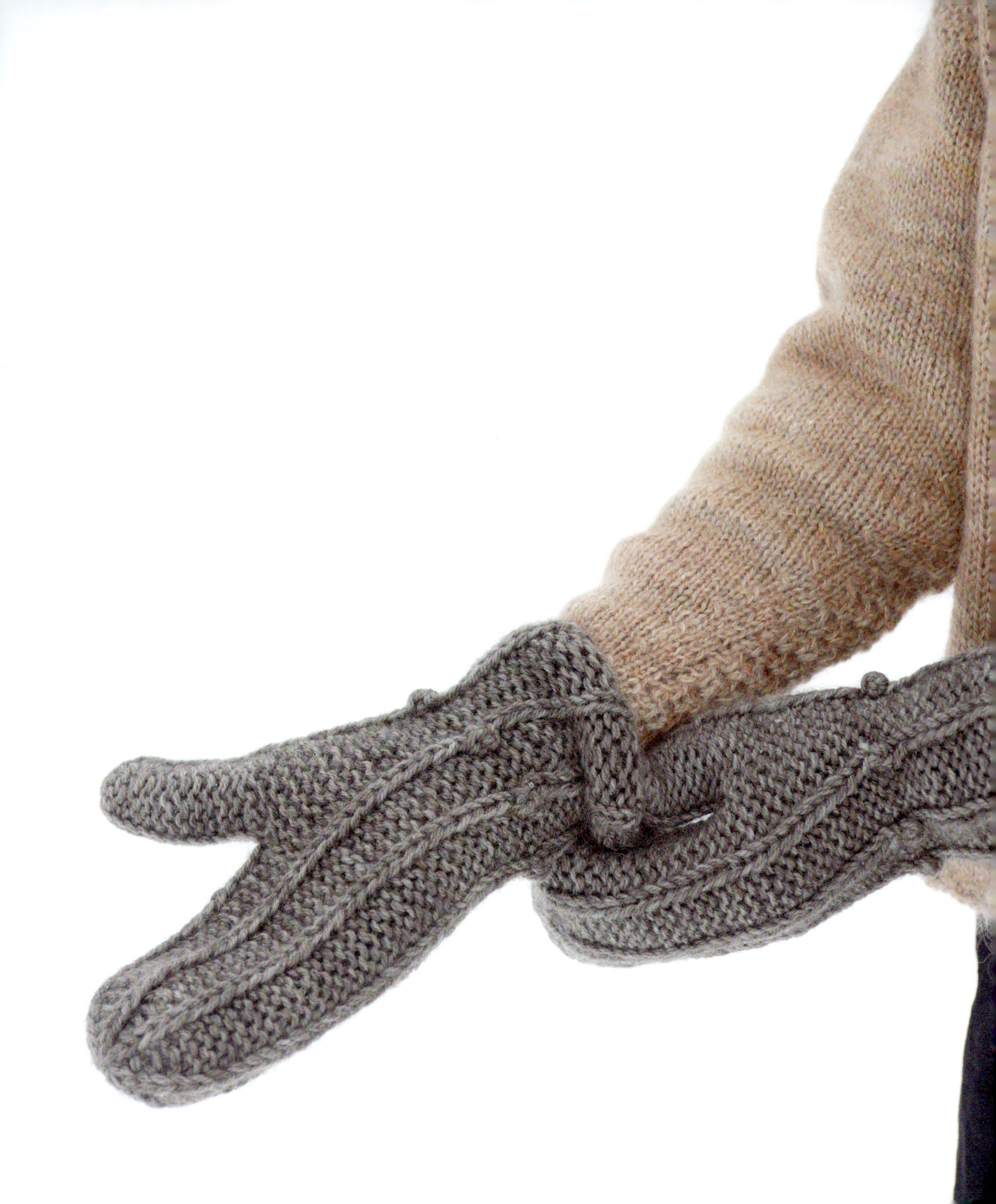

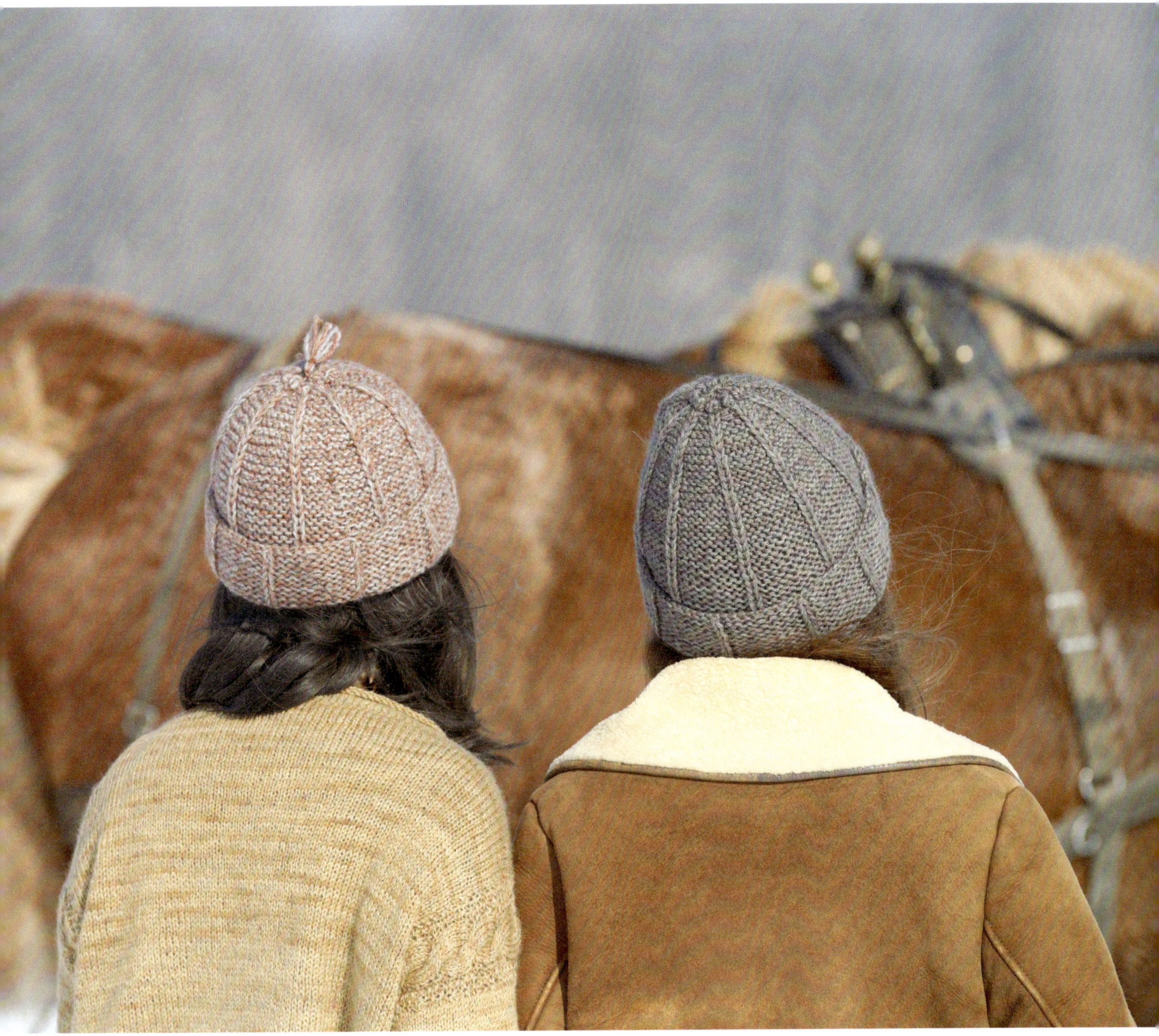

Skyhill Hat + Mitts

Hat
Sizes: 1 (2, 3, 4)
Finished circumference: 42.5 (48, 53.5, 58.5) cm / 17 (19, 21, 23)"
Models both wear size 2.
Mittens
Sizes: 1 (2, 3)
Finished circumference: 18 (20.5, 23) cm / 7 (8, 9)"
Model wears size 1.
Yarn: Viola Shadow DK (DK weight; 50% Polwarth, 35% Wensleydale, 15% Zwartbles; 383 m / 418 yds per 100 g skein)
Shades (Short Hat):
Yarn A: Down to the Wire; 1 skein
Yarn B: Silver Birch; 1 skein
Shades (Tall Hat):
Yarn A: Frozen Earth; 1 skein
Yarn B: Pebble; 1 skein
Shades (Mittens):
Yarn A: Frozen Earth; 1 skein
Yarn B: Pebble; 1 skein
Gauge:
Hat: 19 sts & 32 rounds = 10 cm / 4" over Hat Reversible Columns Pattern on 5 mm needles, with 1 strand each of yarns A and B held together, after blocking
Mittens: 24 sts & 38 rounds = 10 cm / 4" over Mitten Reversible Columns Pattern on 4.5 mm needles, with 1 strand each of yarns A and B held together, after blocking
Needles
Hats: 5 mm / US 8 knitting needles suitable for working small circumferences in the round
Mittens: 4.5 mm / US 7 knitting needles suitable for working small circumferences in the round
Always use a needle size that will result in the correct gauge after blocking.
Notions: 1 stitch marker, 1 locking stitch marker, scrap yarn or stitch holder, tapestry needle
Notes: The Skyhill Hat & Mittens are knit in the round, using slipped sts on the RS and WS of work to create a three-dimensional fabric. Slipped stitches form vertical lines on both the hat and mittens, and are staggered from RS to WS, a smart detail that stands out on the turned up brim of the hat. Bobbles adorn the mitten cuff and crown of the hats and a little optional tassel finishes off the hat. Double stranded Shadow DK is beautiful marled or using two strands of the same colour.

Stitch Glossary

MB (Make Bobble)
Note: Work bobble holding 1 strand each of yarns A and B together.
Row 1 (RS): Kfbf, turn.
Row 2 (WS): P3, turn.
Row 3 (RS): S2kpo.

Hat Reversible Columns (multiple of 10 sts)
Round 1: [P1, k4, sl1 pwise, k4] to end.
Round 2: [Sl1 pwise wyif, p4, k1, p4] to end.
Rep rounds 1-2 for pattern.

Mitten Reversible Columns (multiple of 6 sts)
Round 1: [P1, k2, sl1 pwise, k2] to end.
Round 2: [Sl1 pwise wyif, p2, k1, p2] to end.
Rep rounds 1-2 for pattern.

PATTERN BEGINS
HAT
Using larger needle, long-tail method and holding 1 strand each of yarns A and B together, cast on 80 (90, 100, 110) sts. Join for working in the round, being careful not to twist. PM to indicate beg of round.

Work in Hat Reversible Columns Pattern for 17.5 cm / 7" / 32 garter ridges (SHORT version) OR 21.5 cm / 11½" / 37 garter ridges (TALL version), measured from cast-on edge, ending with a round 2.

Shape Crown
Round 1 (Dec): [P1, k2, ssk, sl1 pwise, k2tog, k2] to end. *64 (72, 80, 88) sts*
Round 2: [Sl1 pwise wyif, p3, k1, p3] to end.
Round 3: [P1, k3, sl1 pwise, k3] to end.

Short Version ONLY: Rep round 2 once more.
Long Version ONLY: Rep rounds 2-3 a further 4 times, then work round 2 once more.

BOTH Versions again
Round 4 (Dec): [P1, k1, ssk, sl1 pwise, k2tog, k1] to end. *48 (54, 60, 66) sts*
Round 5: [Sl1 pwise wyif, p2, k1, p2] to end.
Round 6: [P1, k2, sl1 pwise, k2] to end.

Short Version ONLY: Rep round 5 once more.

Long Version ONLY: Rep rounds 5-6 a further 4 times, then work round 5 once more.
BOTH Versions again
Round 7 (Dec): [P1, ssk, sl1 pwise, k2tog] to end. *32 (36, 40, 44) sts*
Round 8: [Sl1 pwise wyif, p1, k1, p1] to end. Remove beg of round marker.
Round 9 (Dec): P1, k1, PM for new beg of round, [k1, s2kpo] to end. *16 (18, 20, 22) sts*
Round 10: [MB, p1] to end.
Round 11: [K2tog] to end. *8 (9, 10, 11) sts*
Break yarn and thread through rem sts on needle, pulling tight to close.

HAT FINISHING
Make tassel and attach to top of hat. Weave in ends and block to measurements.

MITTENS (make 2)
Cuff
Using smaller needle, long-tail method, and holding 1 strand each of yarns A and B together, cast on 42 (48, 54) sts. Join for working in the round, being careful not to twist. PM to indicate beg of round.

Work Mitten Reversible Columns Pattern for 7.5 cm / 3" / 14 garter ridges, ending with a round 1.
Bobble round: [Sl1 pwise wyif, p2, MB, p2] to end.

Thumb Gusset
Set-up round: P1, k2, PM, cast on 1 st using backwards loop method, sl1 pwise, placing locking stitch marker into slipped st, cast on 1 st using backwards loop method, PM, k2, [p1, k2, sl1 pwise, k2] to end. *44 (50, 56) sts*
Round 1: Sl1 pwise wyif, p2, SM, p to marked st, k marked st, p to marker, SM, p2, [sl1 pwise wyif, p2, k1, p2] to end.
Round 2: P1, k2, SM, k to marked st, sl marked st pwise, k to marker, SM, k2, [p1, k2, sl1 pwise, k2] to end.
Round 3: Rep round 1.
Round 4 (Inc): P1, k2, SM, k to marked st, using backwards loop method, cast on 1 st, sl marked st pwise, using backwards loop method, cast on 1 st, k to marker, SM, k2, [p1, k2, sl1 pwise, k2] to end. *46 (52, 58) sts; 5 thumb sts between markers*
Rounds 5-7: Rep rounds 1-3 once more.
Round 8 (Inc): P1, k2, SM, p1, k to marked st, using backwards loop method, cast on 1 st, sl marked st pwise, using backwards loop method, cast on 1 st, k to 1 st before marker, p1, SM, k2, [p1, k2, sl1 pwise, k2] to end. *2 sts inc*

Round 9: Sl1 pwise wyif, p2, SM, sl1 pwise wyif, p to marked st, k marked st, p to 1 st before marker, sl1 pwise wyif, SM, p2, [sl1 pwise wyif, p2, k1, p2] to end.
Round 10: P1, k2, SM, p1, k to marked st, sl marked st pwise, k to 1 st before marker, p1, SM, k2, [p1, k2, sl1 pwise, k2] to end.
Round 11: Rep round 9.
Rep rounds 7-11 a further 2 (3, 4) times. *52 (60, 68) sts; 11 (13, 15) thumb sts*

Next round (Inc): P1, k2, SM, p1, k2, p1, k1, using backwards loop method, cast on 1 st, sl marked st pwise, using backwards loop method, cast on 1 st, k1, p1, k2, p1, SM, k2, [p1, k2, sl1 pwise, k2] to end. *54 (62, 70) sts; 13 (15, 17) thumb sts*
Next round: Sl1 pwise wyif, p2, SM, [sl1 pwise wyif, p2] twice, k marked st, [p2, sl1 pwise wyif] twice, SM, p2, [sl1 pwise wyif, p2, k1, p2] to end.
Next round: P1, k2, SM, [p1, k2] twice, sl marked st pwise, [k2, p1] twice, SM, k2, [p1, k2, sl1 pwise, k2] to end.

Separate Thumb:
Next round: Sl1 pwise wyif, p2, remove marker, slip next 13 (15, 17) sts to holder, remove marker, using backwards loop method, cast on 3 sts to RH needle, p2, [sl1 pwise wyif, p2, k1, p2] to end. *44 (50, 56) sts*

Next round: P1, k3, sl1 pwise, k3, [p1, k2, sl1 pwise, k2] to end.
Next round (Dec): Sl1 pwise wyif, p1, ssk, k1, k2tog, p1, [sl1 pwise wyif, p2, k1, p2] to end. *42 (48, 54) sts*
Continue working straight in pattern as set for another 16 (17, 18) garter ridges (32 (34, 36) rounds). Work should measure 8.5 (9, 9.5) cm / 3¼ (3½, 3¾)" from top of thumb or 1.5 cm / ½" short of desired length for hand, ending with a pattern round 2 and stopping 2 sts before the end of the round.

Shape Top
Round 1 (Dec): [K1, s2kpo, k1, sl1 pwise] to end. *28 (32, 36) sts*
Round 2: [P1, sl1 wyif, p1, k1] to end.
Round 3: [K1, p1, k1, sl1 pwise] to end.
Round 4: Rep round 2.
Round 5 (Dec): [S2kpo, sl1 pwise] to end. *14 (16, 18) sts*
Round 6: [Sl1 wyif, k1] to end.
Cut yarn and thread tail through rem sts on needle, pulling tight to close.

Thumb
Place 13 (15, 17) held sts onto needle(s).
Round 1: With RS facing, beg at centre top of thumb opening, pick

up and knit 2 sts in last 2 cast-on sts for hand, p0 (1, 2), [sl1 pwise wyif, p2] twice, k1, [p2, sl1 pwise wyif] twice, p0 (1, 2). Pick up and knit 1 st in rem cast-on st. PM to indicate beg of round. *16 (18, 20) sts*
Round 2: Sl1 pwise, k1 (2, 3), [p1, k2] twice, sl1 pwise, [k2, p1] twice], k1 (2, 3).
Round 3: K1, p1 (2, 3), [sl1 pwise wyif, p2] twice, k1, [p2, sl1 pwise wyif] twice, p1 (2, 3).

Size 1 ONLY
Round 4 (Dec): Sl1 pwise, k2tog, k2, p1, k2, sl1 pwise, k2, p1, k2, ssk. *14 sts*
Round 5: K1, p3, sl1 pwise wyif, p2, k1, p2, sl1 pwise wyif, p3.
Round 6 (Dec): Sl1 pwise, k2tog, k1, p1, k2, sl1 pwise, k2, p1, k1, ssk. *12 sts*

Size 2 ONLY
Round 4: *Sl1 pwise, k2, [p1, k2] twice; rep from * once more.
Round 5: *K1, p2, [sl1 pwise wyif, p2] twice; rep from * once more.
Round 6: *Sl1 pwise, k2, [p1, k2] twice; rep from * once more.

Size 3 ONLY
Round 4 (Dec): Sl1 pwise, k2tog, k1, [p1, k2] twice, sl1 pwise, [k2, p1] twice, k1, ssk. *18 sts*
Round 5: K1, p2, [sl1 pwise wyif, p2] twice, k1, [p2, sl1 pwise wyif] twice, p2.
Round 6: Sl1 pwise, k2, [p1, k2] twice, sl1 pwise, [k2, p1] twice, k2.

ALL Sizes Again
Round 1: *K1, p2, [sl1 pwise wyif, p2] 1 (2, 2) times; rep from * once more.
Round 2: *Sl1 pwise, k2, [p1, k2] 1 (2, 2) times; rep from * once more.
Rep rounds 1-2 for 6.5 cm / 2½", ending with round 1.

Shape Top of Thumb
Size 1 ONLY
Round 1 (Dec): [Sl1 pwise, ssk, p1, k2tog] twice. *8 sts*
Round 2: [K1, p3] twice.
Round 3 (Dec): [Sl1 pwise, s2kpo] twice. *4 sts*
Round 4: [Sl1 pwise, p1] twice.

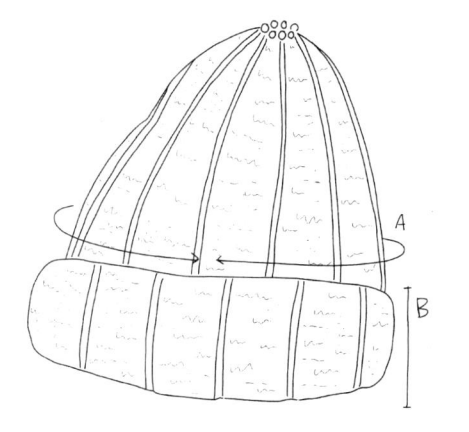

Sizes 2 & 3 ONLY
Round 1 (Dec): [Sl1 pwise, k2, ssk, k2tog, k2] twice. *14 sts*
Round 2: [K1, p6] twice.
Round 3 (Dec): [Sl1 pwise, s2kpo, s2kpo] twice. *6 sts*
Round 4: [Sl1 pwise, p2] twice.

ALL sizes again
Break yarn and thread through rem 4 (6, 6) sts, pulling tight to close.

MITTEN FINISHING
Weave in ends and block to measurements.

Skyhill Hat
A. Finished circumference: 42.5 (48, 53.5, 58.5) cm / 17 (19, 21, 23)"

Tall Hat Length:
B. Brim folded: 21.5 cm / 8½"

Short Hat Length:
B. Brim folded: 17.5 cm / 7"

Skyhill Mitts
A. Finished circumference: 18 (20.5, 23) cm / 7 (8, 9)"
B. Length (cuff to top): 21 (21.5, 22) cm / 8¼ (8½, 8¾)"
C. Thumb length: 6.5 (6.5, 6.5) cm / 2½ (2½, 2½)"

Mitten Reversible Columns

6	5	4	3	2	1	
●	●		●	●	V̇	2
		V			●	1
6	5	4	3	2	1	

Key
- ☐ knit
- ● purl
- V sl1 pwise
- V̇ sl1 pwise wyif

BARN

59

Barn Sweater

As its name might suggest, I designed this jumper with work in mind. Like the Eastwind Jacket, it is loose fitting to allow for layering and mobility. It is long in the body to keep draughts out and has deep armholes that won't pull or bind. It also features an unusual method of construction, which evolved while pondering fence lines in fields. These fence lines at times run parallel, intersect, or change direction completely. From a distance, they appear as a variety of line types and weights travelling across the land, each on their own journey.

61

62

Barn Sweater

Sizes: 1 (2, 3, 4, 5, 6)
Finished bust circumference: 94 (104, 114.5, 124.5, 134.5, 147.5) cm / 37 (41, 45, 49, 53, 58)" – to be worn with 17.5-25.5 cm / 7-10" positive ease
Model has 84 cm / 33" bust, is wearing a size 2, with 20 cm / 8" positive ease.
Yarn: Viola Mooresburg DK (DK weight; 100% Cotswold/Dorset Wool; 238 m / 260 yds per 100 g skein)
Shade: Fireside; 5 (6, 7, 7, 8, 8) skeins
Gauge: 23 sts & 30 rounds = 10 cm / 4" over St st in the round on 4 mm needles, after blocking.
Needles: 4mm / US 6 circular needles, 80 cm / 32" length, **AND** needles suitable for working small circumferences in the round
Always use a needle size that will result in the correct gauge after blocking.
Notions: 6 stitch markers, 6 locking stitch markers, tapestry needle
Notes: Barn Sweater is knit modularly, joining pieces together as the garment is worked. Stitches are cast on for Piece One across the mid back, and the first piece is knit flat from the bottom of the shoulder blades, over the shoulders, to below the bust. Short row shaping is worked across the back to add depth, and the neck opening is formed as Piece One is knit. Stitches are then picked up for Piece Two in the cast-on and cast-off edges of Piece One, and joined to work in the round to form the lower body. Finally, sleeve stitches are picked up along the selvedge edges of Piece One, and knit in the round to the cuffs. A small seam is sewn under the arms before working the sleeves and a ribbed collar finishes off the neck. Please refer to schematics for visual aid, direction of knitting and assembly guidance. When working Piece One, all lengths are measured from either the beginning or end of the row.

Stitch Glossary

1x1 Rib (worked over an odd number of sts)
Row 1 (RS): [K1, p1] to last st, k1.
Row 2 (WS): [P1, k1] to last st, p1.
Rep rows 1-2 for pattern.

1x1 Rib (worked over an even number of sts)
Row 1 (RS): [K1, p1] to end.
Rep row 1 for pattern.

PATTERN BEGINS
PIECE ONE - Back
Using the long-tail method, cast on 159 (171, 187, 199, 215, 227) sts.
Set-up row 1 (WS): Purl.
Set-up row 2 (RS): K26 (26, 28, 28, 30, 30) sts, place locking stitch marker in next st, k107 (119, 129, 141, 153, 167) sts, place locking stitch marker in last st worked, k26 (26, 28, 28, 30, 30).
Note: Locking stitch markers indicate 'underarm' points and are useful when picking up sts for working Piece Two.
Next row (WS): Purl.
Note: Last three rows form St st band into which sts are picked up for working Piece Two.

Ribbed Stripe
Row 1 (RS): Work 1x1 Rib over 73 (79, 87, 93, 101, 107), PM, [p1, k1] 6 times, p1, PM, work 1x1 Rib over 73 (79, 87, 93, 101, 107) sts.
Row 2 (WS): Work all sts as they appear (knit the knits and purl the purls).
Rep rows 1-2 once more, slipping markers as you pass them.

Establish St st Panels
Next row (RS): K to marker, SM, [p1, k1] 6 times, p1, SM, k to end.
St st and centre ribbed panel are established for Back of Piece One. Maintain ribbed panel as set, slipping all markers as you pass them.

Shape Back
Next row (RS): Patt to last 5 sts, w&t.
Next row (WS): Patt to last 5 sts, w&t.
Short row 1 (RS): Patt to 5 sts before w&t, w&t.
Short row 2 (WS): Patt to 5 sts before w&t, w&t.
Repeat Short rows 1-2 a further 10 (10, 11, 11, 12, 12) times, ending with a row 2. *12 (12, 13, 13, 14, 14) sts wrapped at each end of piece*
Next row (RS): Patt to end, concealing wraps as you come to them.
Work straight in patt as established until Back measures 21.5 (21.5, 23, 24, 24, 25.5) cm / 8½ (8½, 9, 9½, 9½, 10)" from cast-on edge at beg or end of row, ending with a WS Row.
Note: Full depth for back is reached, piece will continue onto Front, beginning with neck shaping.

PIECE ONE - Front
Next row (RS): K61 (67, 74, 80, 87, 93) sts for Right neck, cast off 37 (37, 39, 39, 41, 41) sts for Back neck removing markers, k to end. *122 (134, 148, 160, 174, 186) sts*
Place locking stitch markers in first and last sts of previous row. Work each side of neck separately. Place Right neck sts on hold and continue on Left neck only.

Left Neck Shaping
Working back and forth over 61 (67, 74, 80, 87, 93) sts of Left neck, work straight in patt for 2 cm / ¾", ending with a WS row.
Row 1 (RS): K2, M1R, k to end. *1 st inc*
Row 2 (WS): Purl.
Rep rows 1-2 a further 3 times. *65 (71, 78, 84, 91, 97) sts on Left front*

Barn Sweater

Next row (RS): Cast on 2 (2, 2, 2, 3, 3) sts, k to end. *67 (73, 80, 86, 94, 100) sts*
Next row (WS): Purl.
Next row: Cast on 2 (2, 3, 3, 3, 3) sts, k to end. *69 (75, 83, 89, 97, 103) sts*
Next row: Purl.
Next row: Cast on 4 sts, k to end. *73 (79, 87, 93, 101, 107) sts*
Next row: Purl.
Break yarn and place sts on hold for Left front.

Right Neck Shaping
With WS facing, rejoin yarn at neck edge of held Right neck sts. *61 (67, 74, 80, 87, 93) sts*
Work in patt for 2 cm / ¾", ending with a RS Row.
Row 1 (WS): Purl.
Row 2 (RS): K to last 2 sts, M1L, k2. *1 st inc*
Rep rows 1- 2 a further 3 times. *65 (71, 78, 84, 91, 97) sts*
Next row (WS): Cast on 2 (2, 2, 2, 3, 3) sts, p to end. *67 (73, 80, 86, 94, 100) sts*
Next row (RS): Knit.
Next row: Cast on 2 (2, 3, 3, 3, 3) sts, p to end. *69 (75, 83, 89, 97, 103) sts*
Next row: Knit.
Next row (WS): Cast on 4 sts, p to end. *73 (79, 87, 93, 101, 107) sts*

Rejoin Left and Right Fronts
Next row (RS): K to end of Right front, PM, using cable method cast on 13 sts, PM, k to end of Left front. *159 (171, 187, 199, 215, 227) sts*
Re-establish ribbed panel as foll:
Next row (WS): P to marker, SM, [k1, p1] 6 times, k1, SM, p to end.
Continue in patt as set until work measures 21.5 (21.5, 23, 24, 24, 25.5) cm / 8½ (8½, 9, 9½, 9½, 10)" from locking stitch markers placed at neck cast off row, ending with a WS Row.

Front Ribbed Stripe
Row 1 (RS): Work 1x1 Rib over 73 (79, 87, 93, 101, 107) sts, SM, [p1, k1] 6 times, p1, SM, work 1x1 Rib over 73 (79, 87, 93, 101, 107) sts.
Row 2 (WS): Work all sts as they appear (knit the knits and purl the purls).
Rep rows 1-2 once more, slipping markers as you pass them.

Front Band
Next row (RS): Knit.
Next row (WS): Purl.
Cast off all sts loosely, placing locking stitch markers in the first and last sts of centre ribbed panel (between the two rem markers).
PIECE TWO
Piece Two is worked in the round from the top down. Stitches for Piece Two are picked up in the St st bands at beg and end of Piece One.

Pick up stitches on the wrong side of the bands by inserting needle into 'frowning' purl sts one row up from cast-on / cast-off edges.

Next round: Beg at Left Back locking stitch marker, *pick up and knit 47 (53, 59, 65, 71, 77) sts, PM, pick up and knit 13 sts in Back ribbed panel, PM, pick up and knit 47 (53, 59, 65, 71, 77) sts to Right Back locking stitch marker; rep from * across Front. PM to indicate beg of round. *214 (238, 262, 286, 310, 334) sts*

Next round (RS): *K to marker, SM, [p1, k1] 6 times, p1, SM, k to marker, SM; rep from * once more.
Rep last round until piece measures 30.5 cm / 12" from pickup round, ending last round 1 (0, 1, 0, 1, 0) sts before beg of round marker.

Adjust for Hem Rib
Sizes 1, 3 & 5 ONLY: PM for new beg of round.
Sizes 2, 4 & 6 ONLY: Remove marker, k1, PM for new beg of round.

ALL Sizes again:
Rib round: [P2, k2] to marker, SM, [p1, k1] 6 times, p1, SM, [k2, p2] to 2 sts before next marker, k2, SM, [p1, k1] 6 times, p1, SM, [k2, p2] to last 2 sts, k2.
Rep Rib round for a total of 16 rounds or 5 cm / 2".
Cast off all sts in patt.

Sew together cast-on and cast off-edges of Piece One before working sleeve. Seam is worked along the same row that Piece Two sts were picked up in.

SLEEVES
Sleeve sts are picked up along the side edges of Piece One (beg and end of rows) and worked in the round from upper arm to cuff.

Pick up for sleeves: With RS facing, using needles suitable for working small circumferences in the round and beg at underarm seam, pick up and knit 43 (45, 47, 49, 53, 55) sts to locking stitch marker, pick up and knit 43 (45, 47, 49, 53, 55) sts. PM to indicate beg of round. *86 (90, 94, 98, 106, 110) sts*
Knit 3 rounds.

Dec round: K2, k2tog, k to last 4 sts, ssk, k2. *2 sts dec*
Rep Dec round every foll 4th round a further 12 (14, 14, 9, 2, 0) times, then every 3rd rnd 0 (0, 0, 7, 16, 20) times. *60 (60, 64, 64, 68, 68) sts*
Work even until Sleeve measures 20.5 (21.5, 21.5, 23, 23, 23) cm / 8 (8½, 8½, 9, 9, 9)" from Piece One, or approximately 5 cm / 2" short of desired length.

Cuff
Rib round: [K2, p2] to end.
Repeat Rib round for a total of 16 rounds or 5 cm / 2".
Cast off all sts in patt.
Rep for second sleeve.

COLLAR

Collar is worked in the round.
With RS facing, using needles suitable for working small circumferences in the round and beg at back right corner of neck opening, pick up and knit: 12 (12, 13, 13, 14, 14) sts in cast off back neck sts, PM, 13 sts in cast off 1x1 rib sts, PM, 12 (12, 13, 13, 14, 14) sts in remaining cast off sts for back neck, 18 (18, 21, 21, 24, 24) sts down Left front neck, PM, 13 sts in cast on 1x1 rib sts, PM, 18 (18, 21, 21, 24, 24) sts up Right front neck.
PM to indicate beg of round. *86 (86, 94, 94, 102, 102) sts*
Next round: K0 (0, 1, 1, 2, 2), [p2, k2] 3 times, SM, [p1, k1] 6 times, p1, SM, [k2, p2] 7 (7, 8, 8, 9, 9) times, k2, SM, [p1, k1] 6 times, p1, SM, [k2, p2] 4 (4, 5, 5, 6, 6) times, k2 (2, 1, 1, 0, 0).
Rep last round a further 12 times.
Cast off all sts in pattern.

FINISHING

Remove locking stitch markers, weave in all ends and block to measurements.

A. Finished bust circumference: 94 (104, 114.5, 124.5, 134.5, 147.5) cm / 37 (41, 45, 49, 53, 58)"
B. Total length: 52 (52, 53.5, 54.5, 54.5, 56) cm / 20½ (20½, 21, 21½, 21½, 22)"
C: Back neck width: 16.5 (16.5, 17, 17, 18.25, 18.25) cm / 6½ (6½, 6¾, 6¾, 7¼, 7¼)"
D: Armhole depth: 21.5 (21.5, 23, 24, 24, 25.5) cm / 8½ (8½, 9, 9½, 9½, 10)"
E: Front neck depth: 6.5 cm / 2½"
F: Shoulder width: 26.5 (29.5, 32.5, 35.5, 38, 40.5) cm / 10½ (11¾, 12¾, 14, 15, 16)"
G: Upper sleeve: 38 (39.5, 41.5, 43, 47, 49) cm / 15 (15½, 16¼, 17, 18½, 19¼)"
H: Lower sleeve: 26.5 (26.5, 28.5, 28.5, 29, 29) cm / 10½ (10½, 11¼, 11¼, 11½, 11½)"
I: Sleeve length: 26.5 cm / 10½"

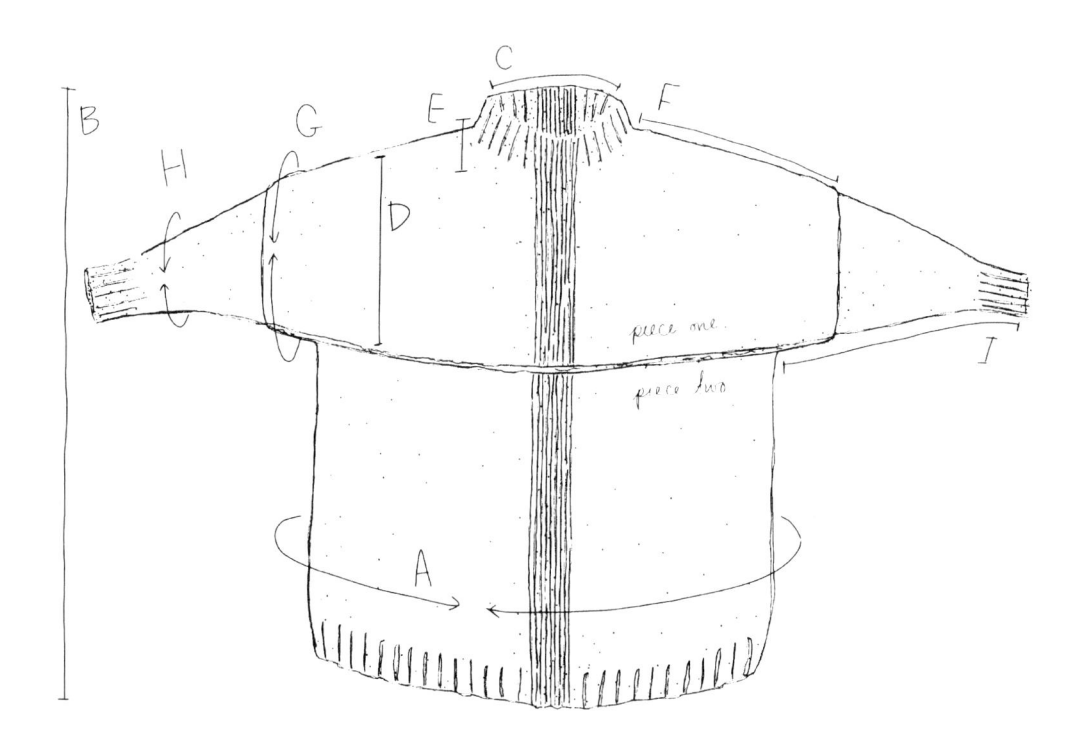

66

FULL MOON

A full moon on a winter's night is right at the top of my list of magical winter experiences. It's no wonder that I found myself knitting these little circles, and even less surprising that I quickly decided they were moons. After a surprisingly short time swatching (how could I improve upon a moon-shaped brioche dot?) I set to work on this pattern with the goal of combining contrasting textures to create a three dimensional, cushioned fabric. Each of those little moons is knit in brioche, and sits on a garter stitch background. However, they occasionally reverse roles to form a tricky optical illusion: the brioche moons move to the background and garter stitch squares appear in the foreground. Whichever shapes you see in this wrap, it is satisfying to knit and very useful when admiring the full moon on a cold night.

68

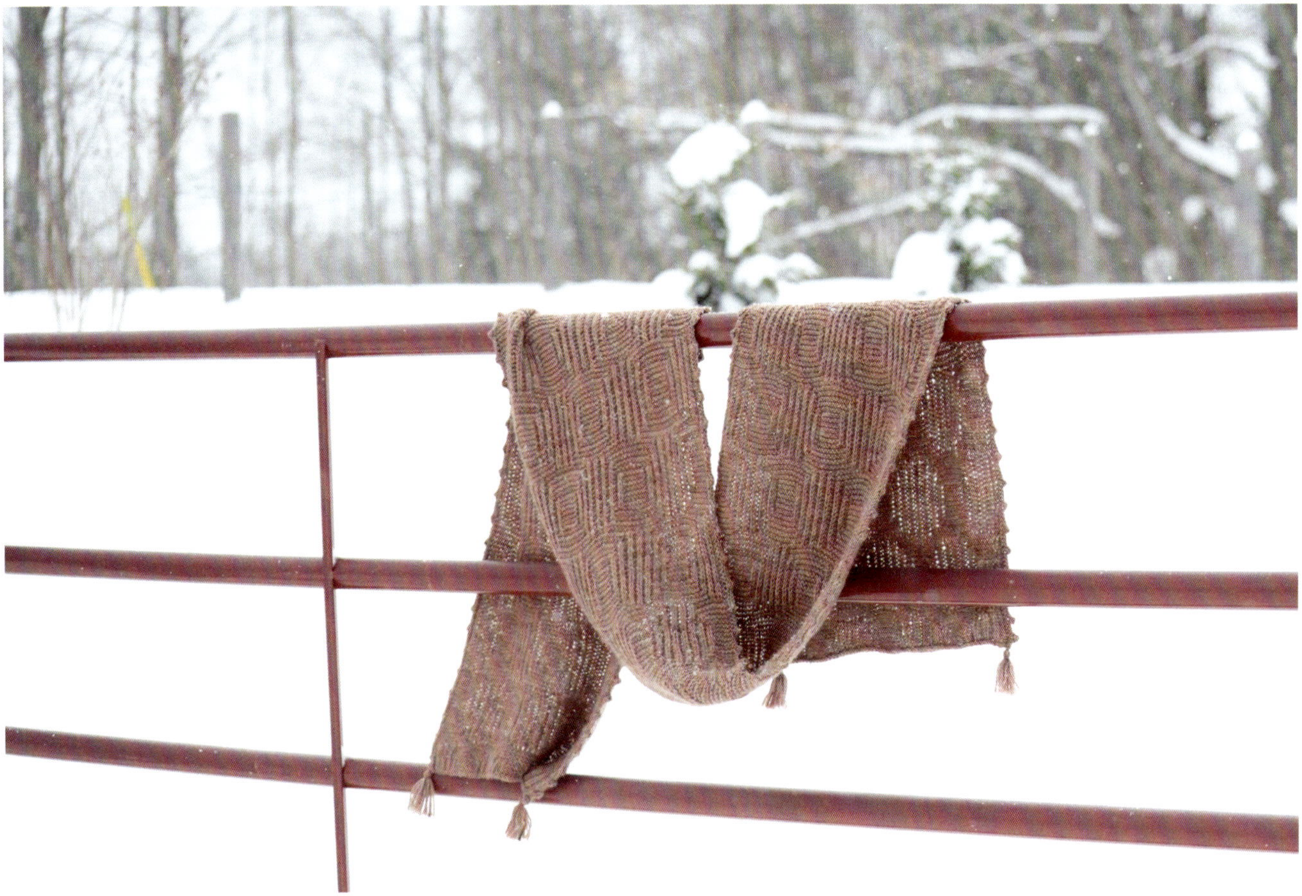

Full Moon

One Size: 213 cm / 84" long x 35.5 cm / 14" wide
Yarn: Viola Shadow DK (DK weight; 50% Polwarth, 35% Wensleydale, 15% Zwartbles; 283 m / 309 yds per 100 g skein)
Shade: Down to the Wire; 4 skeins
Gauge: 19 sts & 38 rows = 10 cm / 4" over Brioche Moon pattern on 4.5 mm needles after blocking
Needles: 4.5 mm / US 7 circular needle, 80 cm / 32" length
Note: Although the shawl is worked flat, a circular needle is recommended due to the large number of sts.
Always use a needle size that will result in the correct gauge after blocking.
Notions: Tapestry needle
Notes: Full Moon Wrap features Brioche 'Moons' evenly spaced on a ground of garter stitch. Don't let the 76-row repeat fool you - this is a simple pattern that is easy to memorise. The Full Moon Wrap is knit in one piece, flat, from end to end. Long sides are finished with a 'Bobble Cast Off' and tassels adorn all four corners.

Stitch Glossary
Bobble Cast Off: [Cast off 4 sts, slip last st worked back to LH needle, kfbf, turn, p3, turn, sk2po] to last 4 sts, cast off to end.

WRITTEN INSTRUCTIONS FOR CHART
(Worked over a multiple of 20 stitches + 6)
Row 1 (RS): K2, *[sl1yo, k1] 4 times, k6, [sl1yo, k1] 3 times; rep from * to last 4 sts, sl1yo, k3.
Row 2 (WS): K2, sl1yo, brk, *[sl1yo, brk] 3 times, k6, [sl1yo, brk] 4 times; rep from * to last 2 sts, k2.
Row 3: K2, *[sl1yo, brk] 4 times, k6, [sl1yo, brk] 3 times; rep from * twice more, sl1yo, brk, k2.
Rows 4-6: Rep rows 2-3 once. Rep row 2 **only** once more.
Row 7: Rep row 3.
Rows 8-10: Rep rows 2-3 once. Rep row 2 **only** once more.
Row 11: K2, *[sl1yo, brk] 3 times, k1, brk, k7, brk, [sl1yo, brk] twice; rep from * to last 4 sts, sl1yo, brk, k2.
Row 12: K2, sl1yo, brk, *[sl1yo, brk] twice, k10, [sl1yo, brk] 3 times; rep from * to last 2 sts, k2.
Row 13: K2, *[sl1yo, brk] 3 times, k10, [sl1yo, brk] twice; rep from * to last 4 sts, sl1yo, brk, k2.
Rows 14-16: Rep rows 12-13 once more. Rep Row 12 **only** once more.
Row 17: K2, *[sl1yo, brk] twice, k1, brk, k11, brk, sl1yo, brk; rep from * to last 4 sts, sl1yo, brk, k2.
Row 18: K2, sl1yo, brk, *sl1yo, brk, k14, [sl1yo, brk] twice; rep from * to last 2 sts, k2.
Row 19: K2, *[sl1yo, brk] twice, k14, sl1yo, brk; rep from * to last 4 sts, sl1yo, brk, k2.
Row 20: Rep row 18.
Row 21: K2, *[k1, brk] twice, k4, [sl1yo, k1] 3 times, k5, brk; rep from * to last 4 sts, k1, brk, k2.
Row 22: K4, *k6, [sl1yo, brk] 3 times, k8; rep from * to last 2 sts, k2.
Row 23: K2, *k8, [sl1yo, brk] 3 times, k6; rep from * to last 4 sts, k4.
Row 24: Rep Row 22.
Row 25: K2, *k6, sl1yo, k1, [sl1yo, brk] 3 times, sl1yo, k5; rep from * to last 4 sts, k4.
Row 26: K4, *k4, [sl1yo, brk] 5 times, k6; rep from * to last 2 sts, k2.
Row 27: K2, *k6, [sl1yo, brk] 5 times, k4; rep from * to last 4 sts, k4.
Rows 28-30: Rep rows 26-27 once. Rep row 28 **only** once more.
Row 31: K2, *k4, sl1yo, k1, [sl1yo, brk] 5 times, sl1yo, k3; rep from * to last 4 sts, k4.
Row 32: K4, *k2, [sl1yo, brk] 7 times, k4; rep from * to last 2 sts, k2.
Row 33: K2, *k4, [sl1yo, brk] 7 times, k2; rep from * to last 4 sts, k4.
Rows 34-44: Rep rows 32-33 five times. Rep row 32 **only** once more.
Row 45: K2, *k5, brk, [sl1yo, brk] 5 times, k1, brk, k2; rep from * to last 4 sts, k4.
Row 46: K4, *k4, [sl1yo, brk] 5 times, k6; rep from * to last 2 sts, k2.
Row 47: K2, *k6, [sl1yo, brk] 5 times, k4; rep from * to last 4 sts, k4.
Rows 48-50: Rep rows 46-47 once. Rep row 46 **only** once more.
Row 51: K2, *k7, brk, [sl1yo, brk] 3 times, k1, brk, k4; rep from * to last 4 sts, k4.
Row 52: K4, *k6, [sl1yo, brk] 3 times, k8; rep from * to last 2 sts, k2.
Row 53: K2, *k8, [sl1yo, brk] 3 times, k6; rep from * to last 4 sts, k4.
Row 54: Rep row 52.
Row 55: K2, *[sl1yo, k1] twice, k5, [brk, k1] 3 times, k3, sl1yo, k1; rep from * to last 4 sts, sl1yo, k1, k2.
Row 56: K2, sl1yo, brk, *sl1yo, brk, k14, [sl1yo, brk] twice; rep from * to last 2 sts, k2.
Row 57: K2, *[sl1yo, brk] twice, k14, sl1yo, brk; rep from * to last 4 sts, sl1yo, brk, k2.
Row 58: Rep row 56.
Row 59: K2, *[sl1yo, brk] twice, sl1yo, k11, sl1yo, k1, sl1yo, brk; rep from * to last 4 sts, sl1yo, brk, k2.
Row 60: K2, sl1yo, brk, *[sl1yo, brk] twice, k10, [sl1yo, brk] 3 times; rep from * to last 2 sts, k2.
Row 61: K2, *[sl1yo, brk] 3 times, k10, [sl1yo, brk] twice; rep from * to last 4 sts, sl1yo, brk, k2.
Rows 62-64: Rep rows 60-61 once. Rep row 60 **only** once more.
Row 65: K2, *[sl1yo, brk] 3 times, sl1yo, k7, sl1yo, k1, [sl1yo, brk] twice; rep from * to last 4 sts, sl1yo, brk, k2.
Row 66: K2, sl1yo, brk, *[sl1yo, brk] 3 times, k6, [sl1yo, brk] 4 times; rep from * to last 2 sts, k2.
Row 67: K2, *[sl1yo, brk] 4 times, k6, [sl1yo, brk] 3 times; rep from * to last 2 sts, sl1yo, brk, k2.
Rows 68-73: Rep rows 66-67 three times.

Row 74: Rep row 66.
Row 75: Rep row 67.
Row 76 (WS): K3, brk, *[k1, brk] 3 times, k6, [k1, brk] 4 times; rep from * to last 2 sts, k2.

PATTERN BEGINS
Using long-tail method, cast on 66 sts. Work 3 rows in St st, beg and ending with a k row.

Following Chart or Written Instructions, work rows 1-74 of Brioche Moon pattern, then rep rows 7-74 a further 11 times or until piece measures desired length.
Work rows 75-76 of Brioche Moon pattern once.

Work 3 rows in St st, beginning and ending with a p row.
Cast off all sts.

Edgings
With RS facing, pick up and knit 308 sts along long edge of piece.
Knit 2 rows.
Work Bobble Cast Off across all sts.
Rep for second long edge.

FINISHING
Make 4 tassels, leaving tails long enough to use for attaching. Weave in all ends, attach tassels to corners, and block to measurements.

A. Length: 213 cm / 84"
B. Width: 35.5 cm / 14"

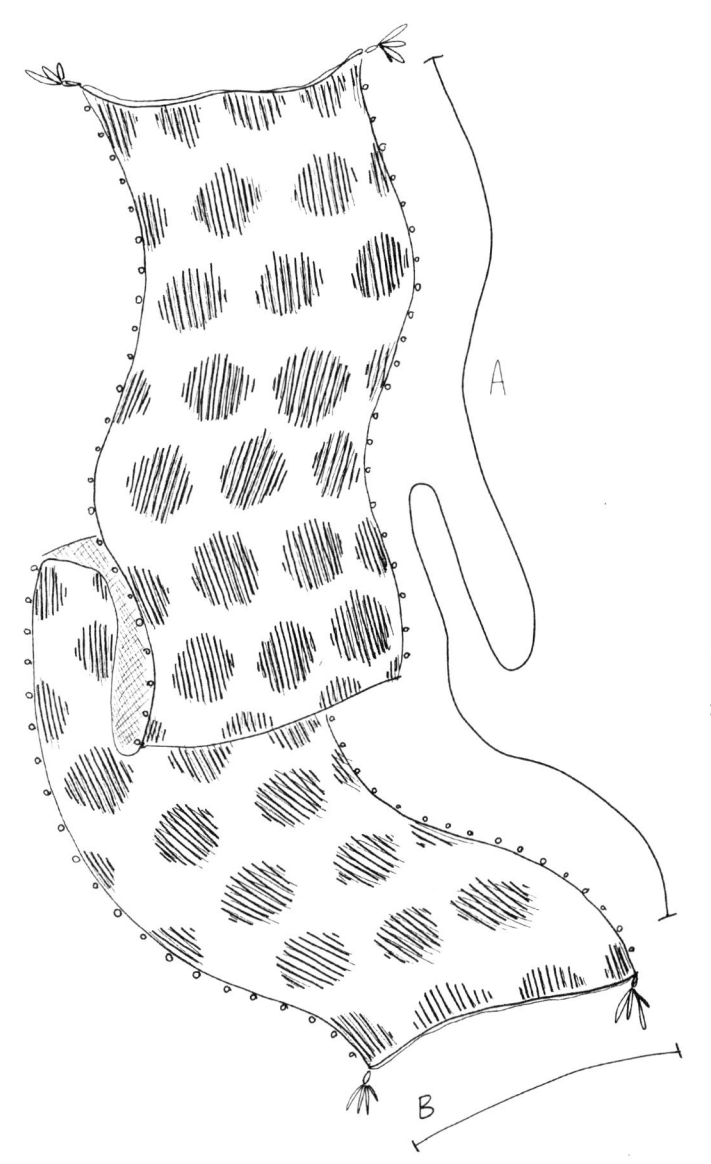

Full Moon

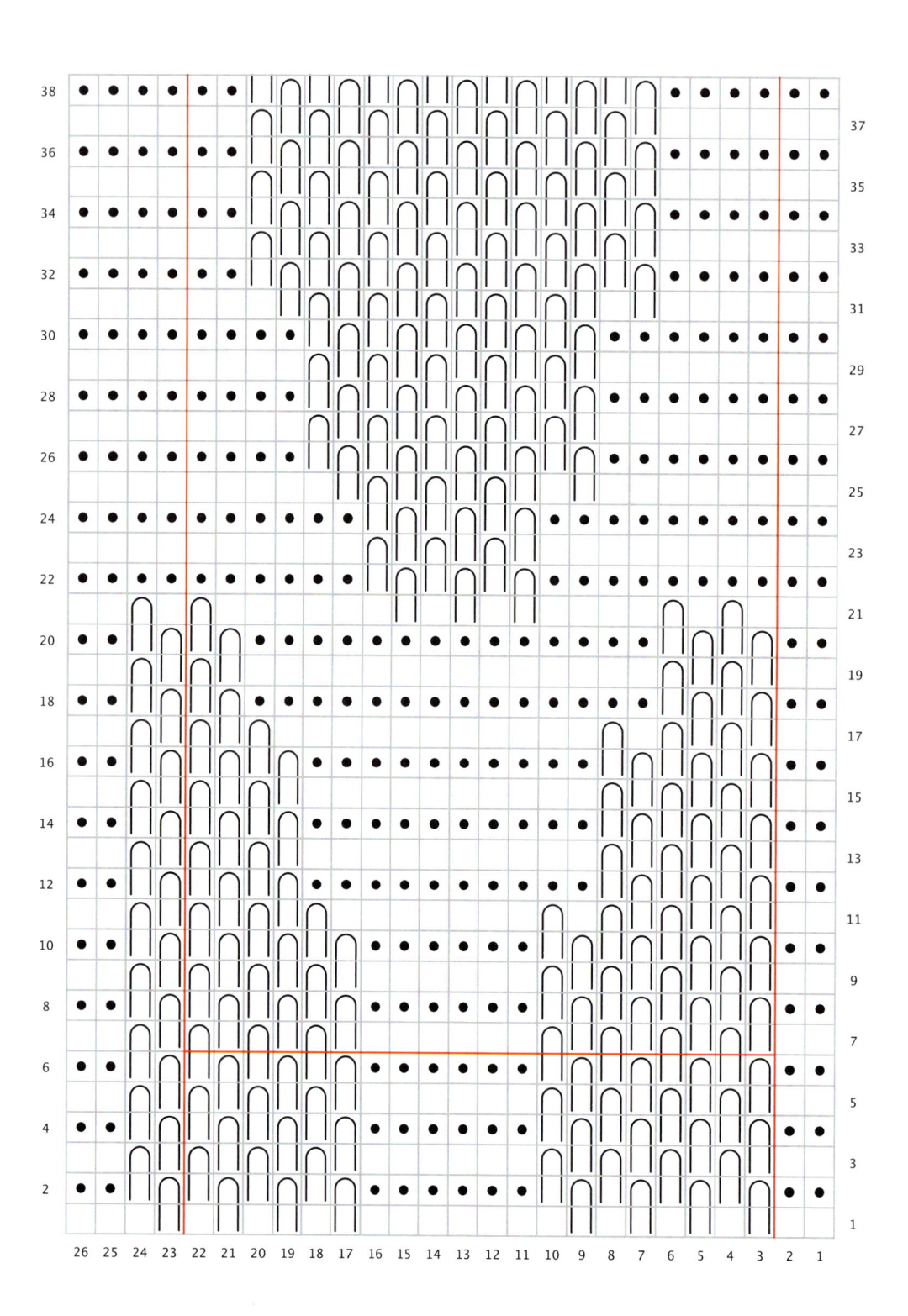

73

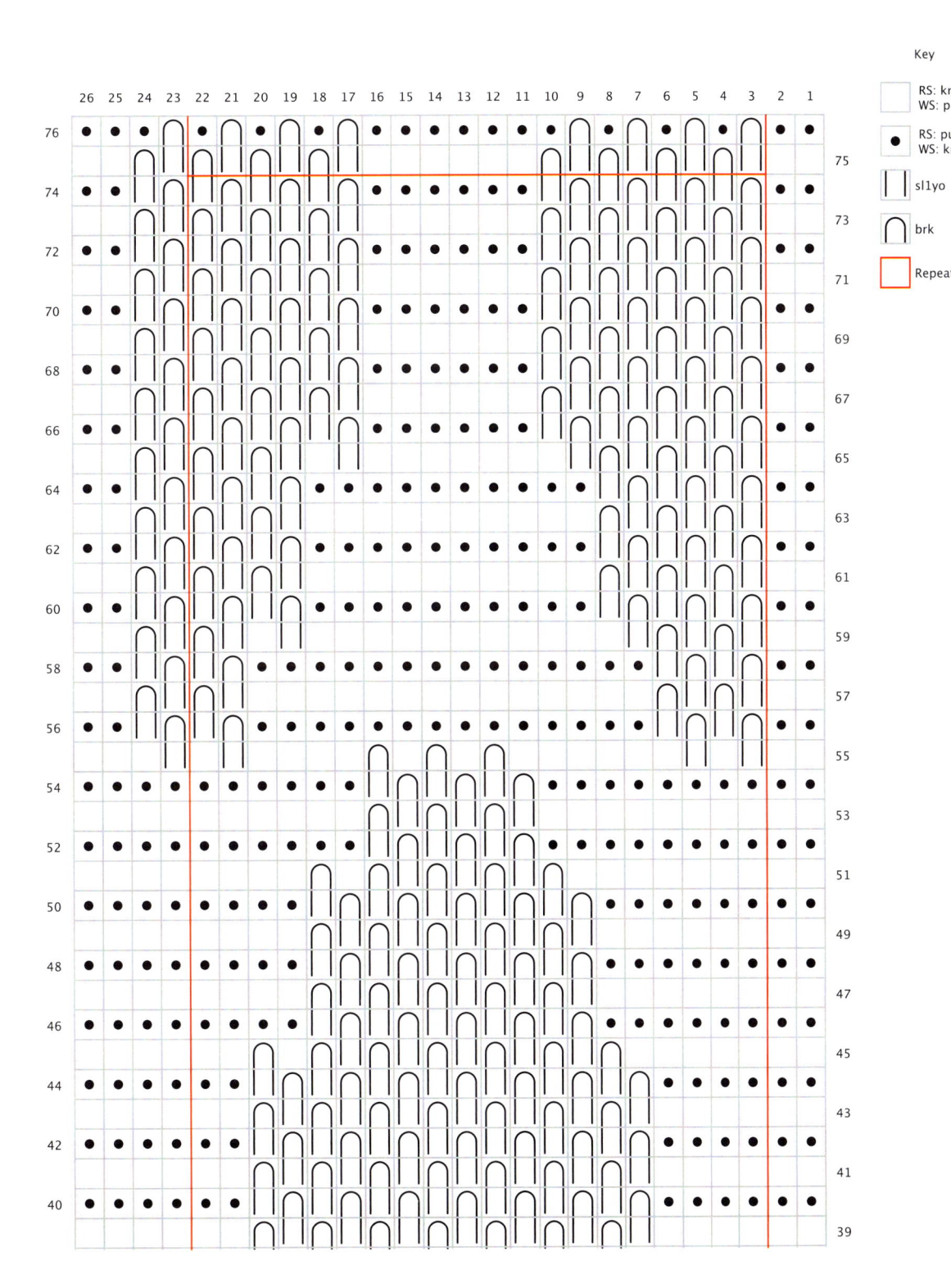

PERSEPHONE

The Persephone Mittens are named after the very special yarn they are knit in, Grey County 4 ply. It's Viola's most local yarn, grown in Keppel Township just down the road and spun a couple of hours south of Mooresburg. The Romney Merino flock that grew this wool live on a farm called Persephone Market Garden, and thus the mittens were named. I knit up the sample pair in the natural grey colour created by the sheep, which I believe to be perfect as it is.

Viola offers small quantities of yarn from this little flock, both dyed and undyed, but these mittens would be beautiful knit in a variety of fingering weight yarns.
I suggest seeking out your own local fibre producer to test out a skein of their 4-ply wool. One quality I always look for when selecting yarn for mittens is durabillity: they need to hold up to a bit of snow shovelling, and this beautiful yarn will do just that. These mittens combine especially well with the Interchangeable Mitten Liners for Very Cold Days (pg 82).

75

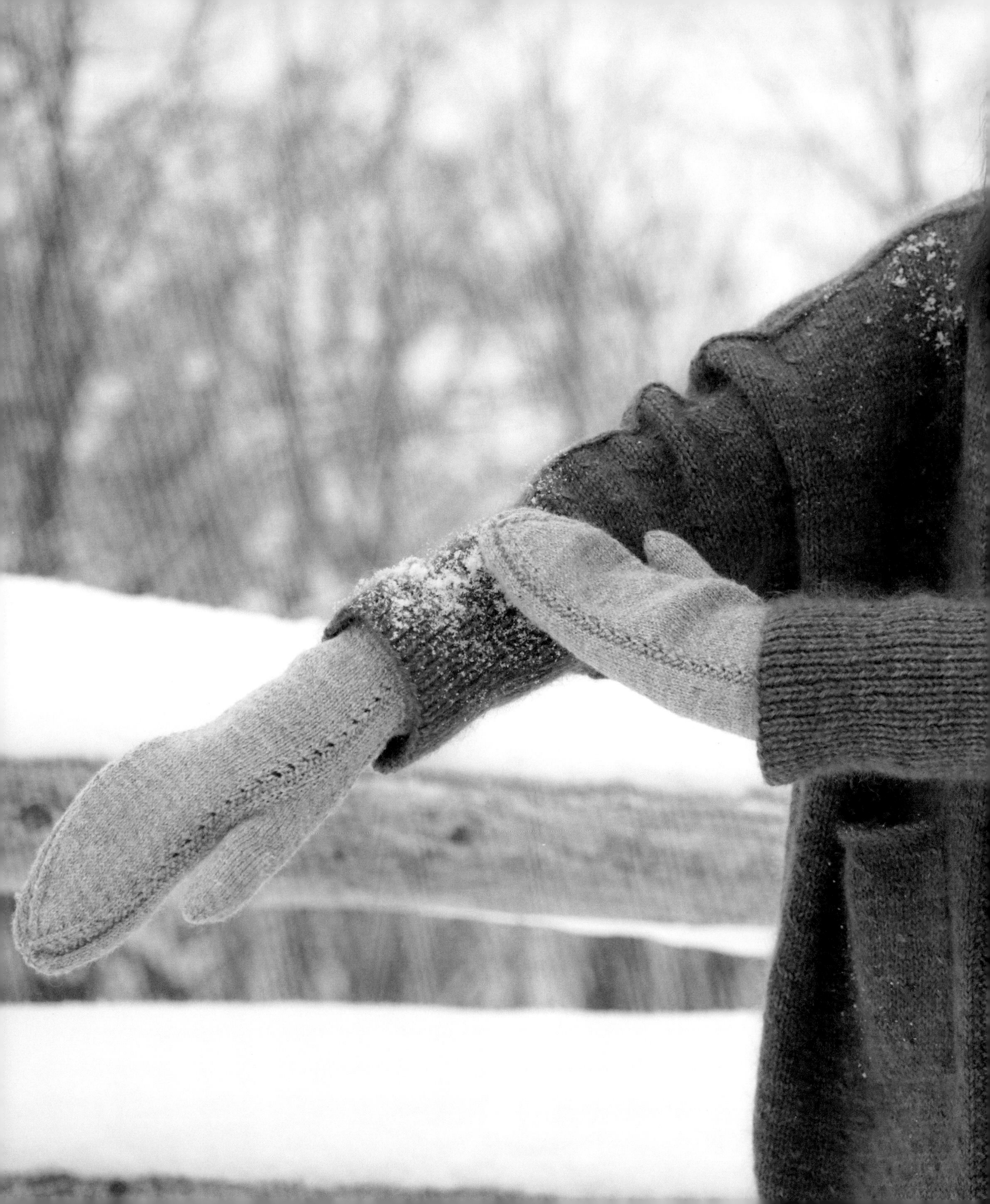

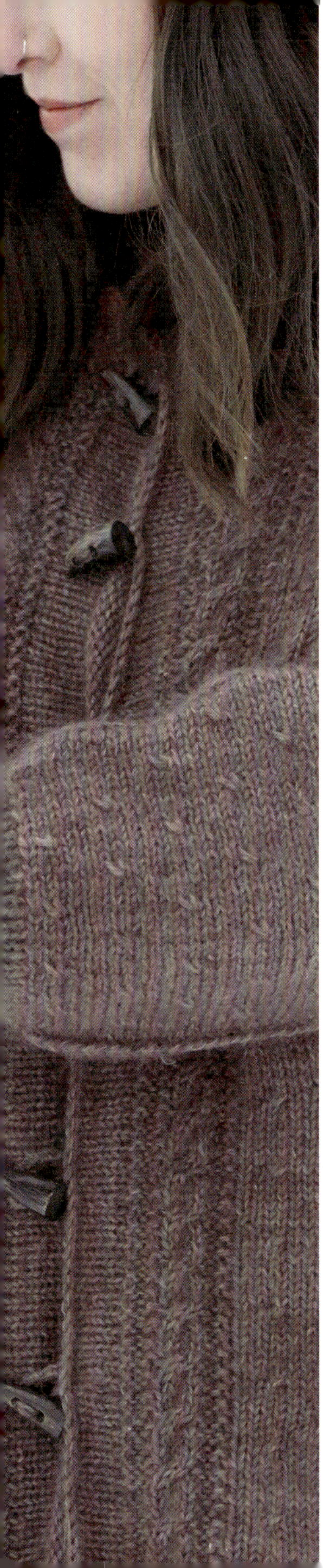
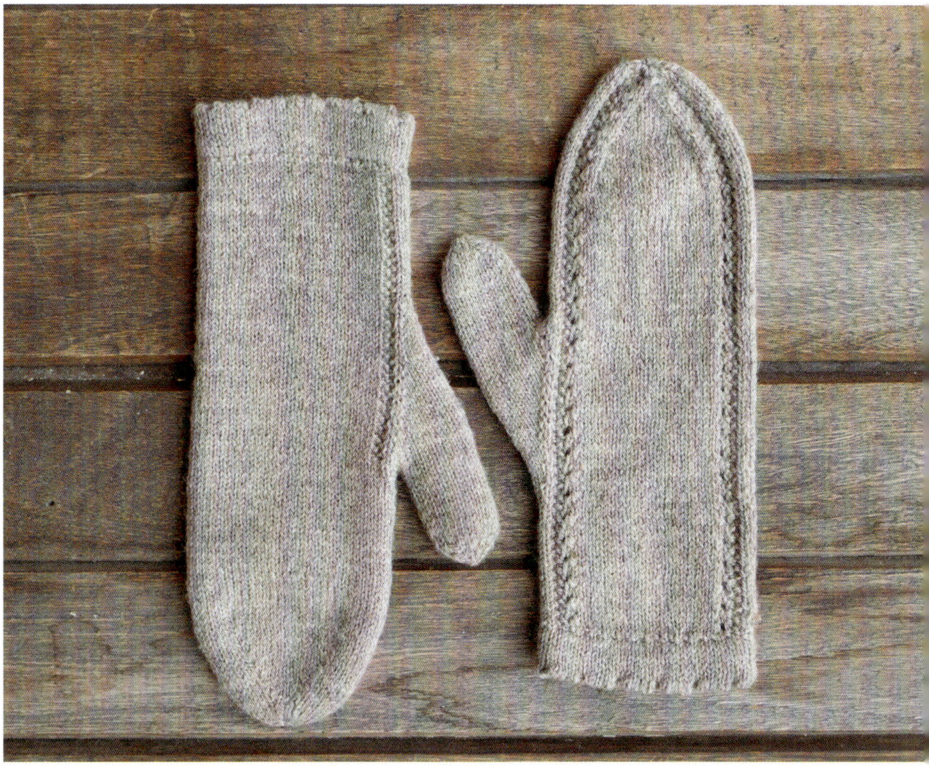

Persephone Mittens

Sizes: 1 (2, 3)
Finished Palm Circumference: 19 (21, 23) cm / 7½ (8¼, 9)" around palm - to be worn with 1-2 cm / ¼ - ¾" positive ease
Model wears size 1.
Yarn: Viola Romney 4ply (4 ply / fingering weight; 100% Romney Merino Wool; 336 m / 368 yds per 100 g skein)
Shade: Natural Grey; 1 skein
Gauge: 32 sts & 48 rounds = 10 cm / 4" over St st in the round on 2.75 mm needles, after blocking
Needles: 2.75 mm / US 2 knitting needles suitable for working small circumferences in the round
Always use a needle size that will result in the correct gauge after blocking.
Notions: 6 stitch markers, cable needle, tapestry needle
Notes: Persephone Mittens are knit from the cuff up with a gusset thumb. A dainty lace pattern outlines the back of the hand, and a subtle column of seed stitch runs up the palm to the top of the thumb. The folded picot Cuff is secured as the mitten is worked by knitting a live st together with a picked up st from cast on edge. If you prefer to use a provisional cast on here, please do.

Stitch Glossary
2/2 RC: Slip 2 sts to cable needle and hold at back, k2, k2 from cable needle.
2/2 LC: Slip 2 sts to cable needle and hold at front, k2, k2 from cable needle.

Tiny Line A (worked over 4 sts)
Round 1: K1, p1, k2.
Round 2: P1, k1, k2.
Round 3: K1, p1, yo, k2tog.
Round 4: P1, k1, k2.
Rep rounds 1-4 for pattern.

Tiny Line B (worked over 4 sts)
Round 1: K2, p1, k1.
Round 2: K3, p1.
Round 3: Ssk, yo, p1, k1.
Round 4: K3, p1.
Rep rounds 1-4 for pattern.

Tiny Line C (worked over 2 sts)
Round 1: K1, p1.
Round 2: P1, k1.
Rounds 3-4: Rep rounds 1-2.
Rep rounds 1-4 for pattern.

PATTERN BEGINS
Cuff – Both Mittens
Using long-tail method, cast on 60 (65, 70) sts. Join for working in the round, being careful not to twist sts. PM to indicate beg of round.

Knit 9 rounds.
Next round (Picot, RS): [K3, yo, k2tog] to end.
Knit 9 rounds.
Next round (Join picot): Fold cuff edge of knitting inside sts on needles, k2tog (1 st on needle with 1 st picked up from cast-on edge) around.
Next round: [K1, p1] to end, increasing 0 (1, 2) sts evenly across the round. *60 (66, 72) sts*

RIGHT MITTEN
Establish Pattern
Round 1: K2, PM, work Round 2 of Tiny Line C, k28 (31, 34), work Round 2 of Tiny Line A, k18 (21, 24), work Round 2 of Tiny Line B, PM, k2.
Round 2: K2, SM, work next round of Tiny Line C, k28 (31, 34), work next round of Tiny Line A, k18 (21, 24), work next round of Tiny Line B, SM, k2.
Continue in patt as est in round 2 for a further 25 rounds (6 full pattern repeats), ending with a round 4 of Tiny Line patterns. Work should measure approx. 7.5 cm / 3" from folded edge.

Shape Thumb Gusset
Round 1 (Inc): K to 1 st before marker, M1L, k1, SM, patt to marker, SM, k1, M1R, k to end. *2 sts inc*
Rounds 2-4: K to marker, SM, patt to marker, SM, k to end.
Continuing in patt, rep rounds 1-4 a further 3 times, then rounds 1-2 **only** 8 (9, 10) times. *84 (92, 100) sts*

Separate Thumb
Next round: Patt to last marker of round, SM, k2, slip next 12 (13, 14) sts to scrap yarn or holder, slip 12 (13, 14) sts from beg of next round to same holder. Using backwards loop method, cast on 1 st to right needle, PM for new beg of round, cast on 1 st. *62 (68, 74) sts*
Tiny Line C ends at top of thumb gusset. These sts are worked in St st from here to end of mitten.

Hand
Next round: K to marker and remove it, k30 (33, 36), PM, work Tiny Line A, k18 (21, 24), work Tiny Line B, SM, k to end.
Next round: K to marker, SM, patt to marker, SM, k to end.
Next round (Dec): K1, k2tog, patt to last 3 sts, ssk, k1. *60 (66, 72) sts*

Continue straight in patt as set for 8 full repeats of Tiny Lines A & B, ending with a round 4. Hand should measure approx. 7 cm / 3" from top of thumb gusset OR 4.5 cm / 1¾" short of desired length.

Shape Mitten Top
Set-up round: K6, PM, k2tog, k14 (17, 20), ssk, PM, k8, SM, work round 1 of Tiny Line, PM, ssk, k14 (17, 20), k2tog, PM, work round 1 of Tiny Line B, SM, k2. *56 (62, 68) sts*

Size 1 & 3 ONLY
Round 1: Patt to end, slipping markers.
Size 2 ONLY
Round 1: [Patt to marker, SM, k2tog, patt to marker, SM] twice, work to end. *60 sts*

ALL Sizes again
Work 2 rounds straight in patt.
Next round (Dec): Patt to marker, SM, k2tog, patt to 2 sts before next marker, ssk, SM, patt to marker, remove marker, patt to marker, SM, ssk, patt to 2 sts before next marker, k2tog, SM, patt to marker, remove marker, patt to end. *52 (56, 64) sts*
Work 3 rounds even.
Next round (Dec): Patt to marker, SM, k2tog, patt to 2 sts before next marker, ssk, SM, patt to marker, SM, ssk, patt to 2 sts before marker, k2tog, SM, patt to end. *4 sts dec*
Continuing in patt, rep last Dec round every 2nd round a further 4 (5, 7) times. *32 sts*
Work 1 round straight in patt after last Dec round.

Next round (Dec): K to marker, remove marker, k2tog, ssk, remove marker, k to 4 sts before marker, k1, p1, k2, remove marker, ssk, k2tog, remove marker, k3, p1, k to end. *28 sts*
Next round: Patt to end.
Next round (Dec): [K2tog] twice, k6, [ssk] twice, [k2tog] twice, k1, 2/2 RC, k1, [ssk] twice. *20 sts*
Next round: Knit.
Next round (Dec): [K2tog, k1, ssk] 4 times. *12 sts*
Break yarn and thread through remaining sts on needle, drawing tight to finish.

LEFT MITTEN
Establish Pattern
Round 1: K2, PM, work Round 2 of Tiny Line A, k18 (21, 24), work Round 2 of Tiny Line B, k28 (31, 34), work Round 2 of Tiny Line C, PM, k2.
Round 2: K2, SM, work next round of Tiny Line A, k18 (21, 24), work next round of Tiny Line B, k28 (31, 34), work next round of Tiny Line C, SM, k2.
Continue in patt as est in round 2 for a further 25 rounds (6 full pattern repeats), ending with a round 4 of Tiny Line patterns. Work should measure approx. 7.5 cm / 3" from folded edge.

Shape Gusset
Work Gusset Shaping as for Right Mitten. *84 (92, 100) sts*
Separate thumb sts and rejoin for hand as for Right Mitten. *62 (68, 74) sts*

Hand
Next round: K to marker, SM, work Tiny Line A, k18 (21, 24), work Tiny Line B, PM, k to marker, remove marker, k to end.
Next round: K to marker, SM, patt to marker, SM, k to end.
Next round (Dec): K1, k2tog, patt to last 3 sts, ssk, k1. *60 (66, 72) sts*
Continue in pattern as set for 8 full repeats of Tiny Line A & B, ending with a round 4. Hand should measure approx. 7 cm / 3" from top of thumb gusset OR 4.5 cm / 1¾" short of desired length.

Shape Mitten Top
Set-up round: K to marker, SM, work round 1 of Tiny Line A, PM, ssk, k14 (17, 20), k2tog, PM, work round 1 of Tiny Line B, SM, k8, PM, k2tog, k14 (17, 20), ssk, PM, k6. *56 (62, 68) sts*

Size 1 & 3 ONLY
Round 1: Patt to end, slipping markers.
Size 2 ONLY
Round 1: [Patt to marker, SM, k2tog, patt to marker, SM] twice, work to end. *60 sts*

ALL Sizes again
Work 2 rounds straight in patt.
Next round (Dec): Patt to marker, remove marker, patt to marker, SM, ssk, patt to 2 sts before next marker, k2tog, SM, patt to marker, remove marker, patt to marker, SM, k2tog, k to 2 sts before next marker, ssk, SM, patt to end. *52 (56, 64) sts*
Work 3 rounds even.
Next round (Dec): Patt to marker, SM, ssk, patt to 2 sts before next marker, k2tog, SM, patt to marker, SM, k2tog, patt to 2 sts before marker, ssk, SM, patt to end. *4 sts dec*
Continuing in patt, rep last Dec round on foll 2nd round once more, then every 2nd round a further 4 (5, 7) times. *32 sts*
Work 1 round straight in patt after last Dec round.

Next round (Dec): K to 4 sts before marker, k1, p1, k2, remove marker, ssk, k2tog, remove marker, k3, p1, k to marker, remove marker, k2tog, ssk, remove marker, k to end. *28 sts*

Persephone Mittens

Next round: Patt to end.
Next round (Dec): [K2tog] twice, k1, 2/2 LC, k1, [ssk] twice, [k2tog] twice, k6, [ssk] twice. *20 sts*
Next round: Knit.
Next round (Dec): [K2tog, k1, ssk] 4 times. *12 sts*
Break yarn and feed tail through remaining sts on needle to finish.

Thumbs (both alike)
Place 24 (26, 28) held thumb sts on needle, and distribute evenly for working in the round. Beg of round is centre top of thumb hole opening.

Round 1: Beg at right edge of cast on sts, pick up and knit 2 sts from cast-on, PM for beg of round, pick up and knit 2 sts from cast-on, knit to end of round. *28 (30, 32) sts*
Round 2: Knit.
Round 3: K1, k2tog, k to last 3 sts, ssk, k1. *26 (28, 30) sts*
Rep rounds 2-3 a further 1 (2, 1) times. *24 (24, 28) sts*
Work straight in patt until thumb measures 5 (6, 7) cm / 2¼ (2½, 2¾)" from base. Shaping adds approximately 1 cm / ¼" to total length for thumb.

Shape Thumb Top
Round 1 (Dec): [K4 (4, 5), k2tog] 4 times. *20 (20, 24) sts*
Round 2: Knit.
Round 3 (Dec): [K3 (3, 4), k2tog] 4 times. *16 (16, 20) sts*
Round 4 (Dec): [K2 (2, 3), k2tog] 4 times. *12 (12, 16) sts*
Round 5 (Dec): [K1 (1, 2), k2tog] 4 times. *8 (8, 12) sts*

Size 3 ONLY
Round 6 (Dec): [K1, k2tog] 4 times. *8 sts*
Break yarn and thread through remaining sts on needle, drawing tight to finish.
Repeat instructions for second Thumb.

FINISHING
Weave in ends and block to measurements.

A. Palm circumference: 19 (21, 23) cm / 7½ (8¼, 9)"
B. Length (cuff to top): 26 (26.5, 27) / 10¼ (10½, 10¾)"
C. Thumb length: 6 (7, 8) cm / 2½ (2¾, 3)"

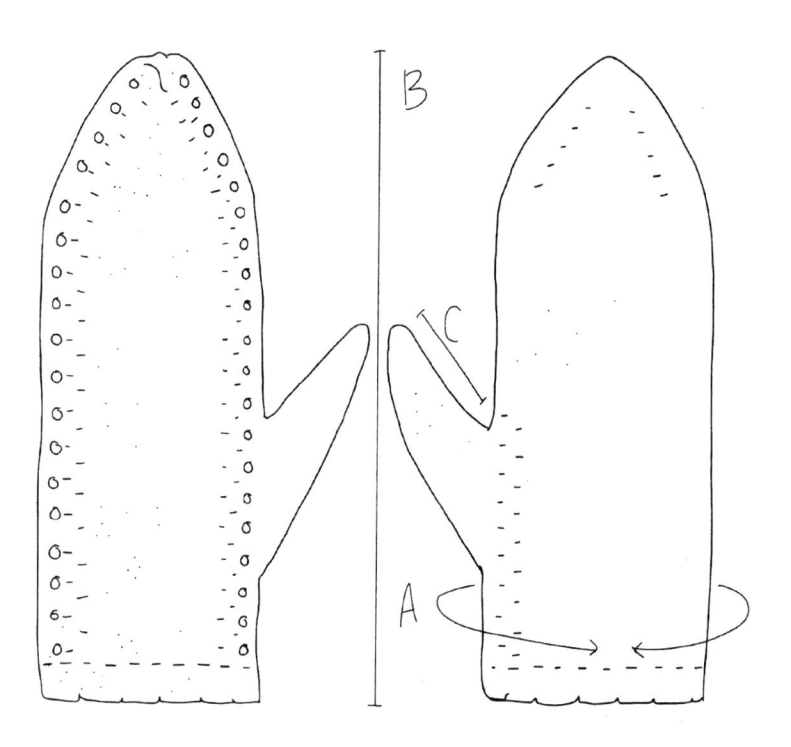

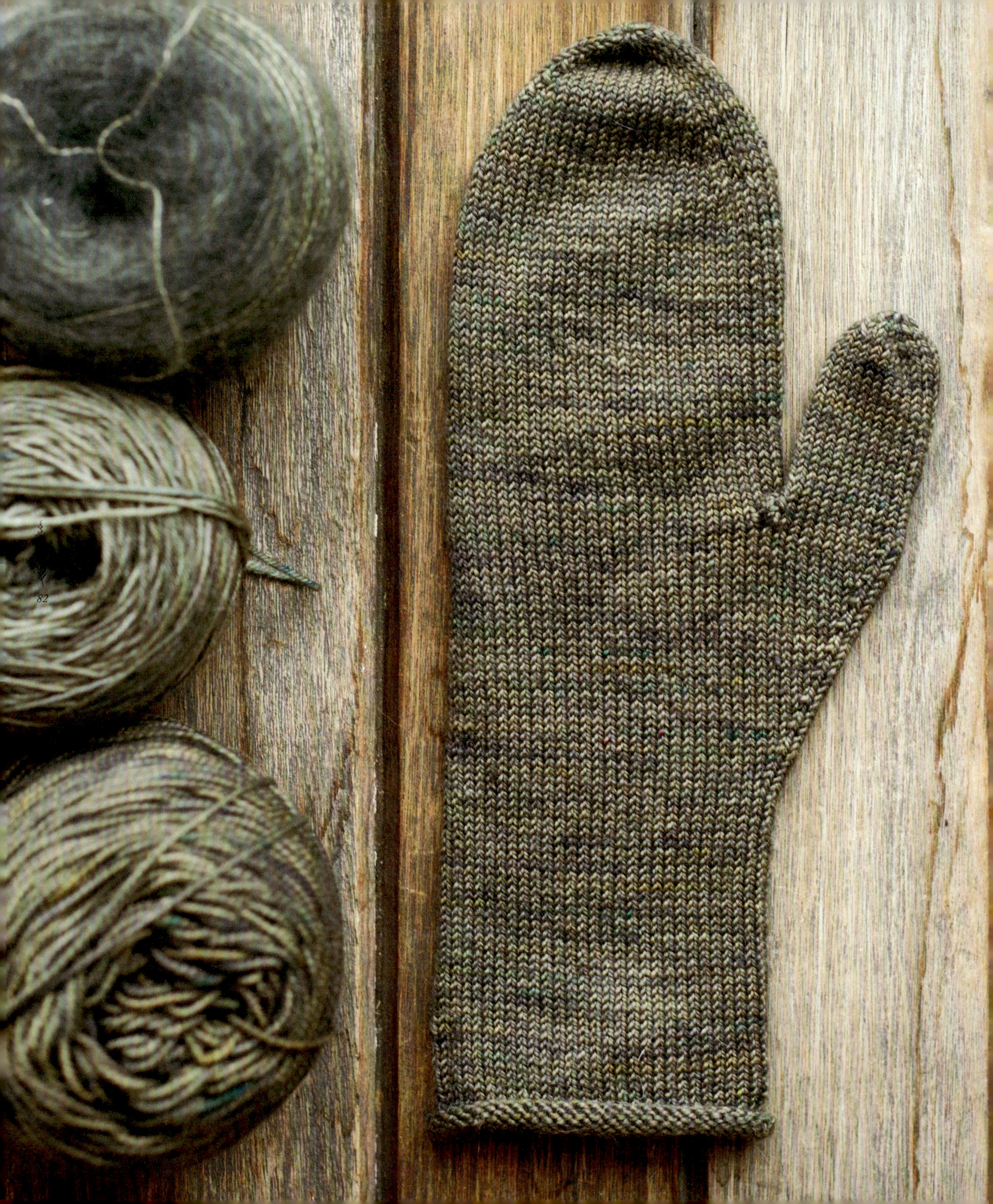

interchangeable MITTEN LINERS for very cold days

I believe these simple mitten liners may be one of the most useful patterns in this book. Throughout winter I am forever doubling up layers of mittens on cold days, yet longing to change out colours or remove a layer for quick drying. You'll have these liners knit in no time, and they're a great way to use up odd skeins of fingering weight yarn (we all have that odd lonely skein lingering in our stash), or you can make a striped pair with sock leftovers. Using up bits, making do and keeping warm is what these mitten liners are all about.

Persephone (pg. 74) pairs especially well with them and its tiny lace detail allows the liners to quietly peek through. Both Persephone and these Liners are knit in fingering weight yarn, so the two layers combined remain lightweight yet warm, not to mention they fit together like… a mitten! On the coldest of days, pop these liners on under the Skyhill Mittens and wander the snowy woods without a care.

Interchangable Mitten Liners

Sizes: 1 (2, 3)
Finished Palm Circumference: 16 (16.5, 18.5) cm / 6¼ (6½, 7¼)"
Model wears size 1.
Yarn: Viola Merino Fingering (4 ply / fingering weight; 100% Superwash Merino; 366 m / 400 yds per 100 g skein)
Shade: Evergreen; 1 skein
Note: A pair of mitten liners uses approx. 50g.
Gauge: 36 sts & 50 rounds = 10 cm / 4" over St st in the round on 2.5 mm needles, after blocking
Needles: 2.5 mm / US 1.5 knitting needles suitable for working small circumferences in the round
Always use a needle size that will result in the correct gauge after blocking.
Notions: 2 stitch markers, scrap yarn or stitch holder, tapestry needle
Notes: These mitten liners are knit entirely in Stocking stitch from the cuff to tip, with a gusset thumb. Plain and simple.

PATTERN BEGINS (make 2 alike)

Cuff
Using the long-tail method, cast on 56 (60, 64) sts. Join for working in the round being careful not to twist sts. PM to indicate beg of round. Work in St st in the round until piece measures 9 cm / 3¾" from cast-on edge.

Shape Thumb Gusset
Round 1 (Inc): K1, cast on 1 st using backward loop method, k to last 2 sts, cast on 1 st using backwards loop method, k1. *2 sts inc*
Rounds 2-3: Knit.
Rep rounds 1-3 a further 8 (9, 10) times. Rep rounds 1-2 **only** once more. *76 (82, 88) sts*

Separate Thumb
Next round: K to last 11 (12, 13) sts of round, slip next 11 (12, 13) sts to scrap yarn or holder, slip 11 (12, 13) sts from beg of next round to same holder. Using backwards loop method, cast on 2 sts to RH needle, PM for new beg of round, cast on 2 sts. *22 (24, 26) held thumb sts; 58 (62, 66) sts*
Next round: Knit.
Next round (Dec): K1, k2tog, k to last 3 sts, ssk, k1. *56 (60, 64) sts*

Hand
Continue in St st until piece measures 8.5 cm / 3¼" from thumb opening, or 4.5 (5. 5.5) cm / 1¾ (2, 2¼)" short of desired total length. On final round, place second marker for shaping as foll: K28 (30, 32), PM, k to end.

Shape Mitten Top
Round 1 (Dec): [K2, k2tog, k to 4 sts before marker, ssk, k2] twice. *4 sts dec*
Rounds 2-4: Knit.
Rep rounds 1-4 once more, then rounds 1-2 **only** once more. *40 (44, 48) sts*

Rep rounds 1-2 a further 7 (8, 9) times. *12 sts*
Break yarn and thread tail through rem sts on needle, pulling tight to close.

Thumb
Place 22 (24, 26) held sts for thumb on needles and distribute evenly.
Round 1: Beg at RS edge of cast-on sts, pick up and knit 2 sts from cast-on, PM for beg of round, pick up and knit 2 sts from cast-on, k across held thumb sts, k to end of round. *26 (28, 30) sts*
Round 2: K1, k2tog, k to last 3 sts, ssk, k1. *24 (26, 28) sts*

Size 2 ONLY
Rep round 2 once more. *24 sts*

ALL Sizes again
Work in St st until thumb measures 5 (5.5, 6.5) cm / 2 (2¼, 2½)" from base or until 1 cm / ¼" short of desired length for Thumb.

Shape Thumb Top
Round 1 (Dec): [K4 (4, 5), k2tog] 4 times. *20 (20, 24) sts*
Round 2: Knit.
Round 3 (Dec): [K3 (3, 4), k2tog] 4 times. *16 (16, 20) sts*
Round 4 (Dec): [K2 (2, 3), k2tog] 4 times. *12 (12, 16) sts*
Round 5 (Dec): [K1 (1, 2), k2tog] 4 times. *8 (8, 12) sts*

Size 3 ONLY
Round 6 (Dec): [K1, k2tog] 4 times. *8 sts*

ALL Sizes again
Break yarn and thread through rem sts on needle, pulling tight to close.

Repeat instructions for second Thumb.

FINISHING
Weave in ends and block to measurements.

A. **Palm circumference:** 16 (17, 18.5) cm / 6¼ (6¾, 7¼)"
B. **Length (cuff to top):** 28 (28.5, 29) cm / 11 (11¼, 11½)"
C. **Thumb length:** 6 (6.5, 7.5) cm / 2¼ (2½, 2¾)"

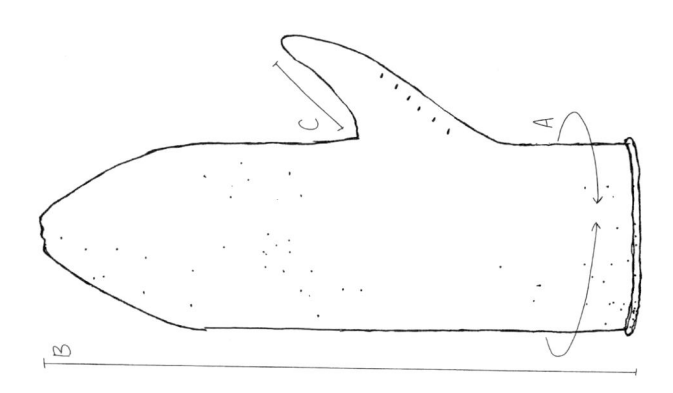

85

Soirée

Originally published in Pom Pom Quarterly's 5th anniversary issue in May 2017, Soirée is back with a few updates. I intended Soirée to be a careful combination of all of my favourite things, and I must have done a decent job because it's still one of my favourite jumpers! It seems fitting that Soirée is reappearing in the winter setting of this book, because I came up with the idea and design last winter. I can remember knitting through a terrible winter flu, when I soon learned the risks of knitting with a fever and had to rip back some very silly mistakes in the original sample! Though I didn't realise it at the time, I'm sure that a little bit of my winter love slipped into this cosy little jumper. I still think it's the perfect jumper for a party and am certain that the hard-working settlers of Mooresburg enjoyed a soirée or two in their day!

87

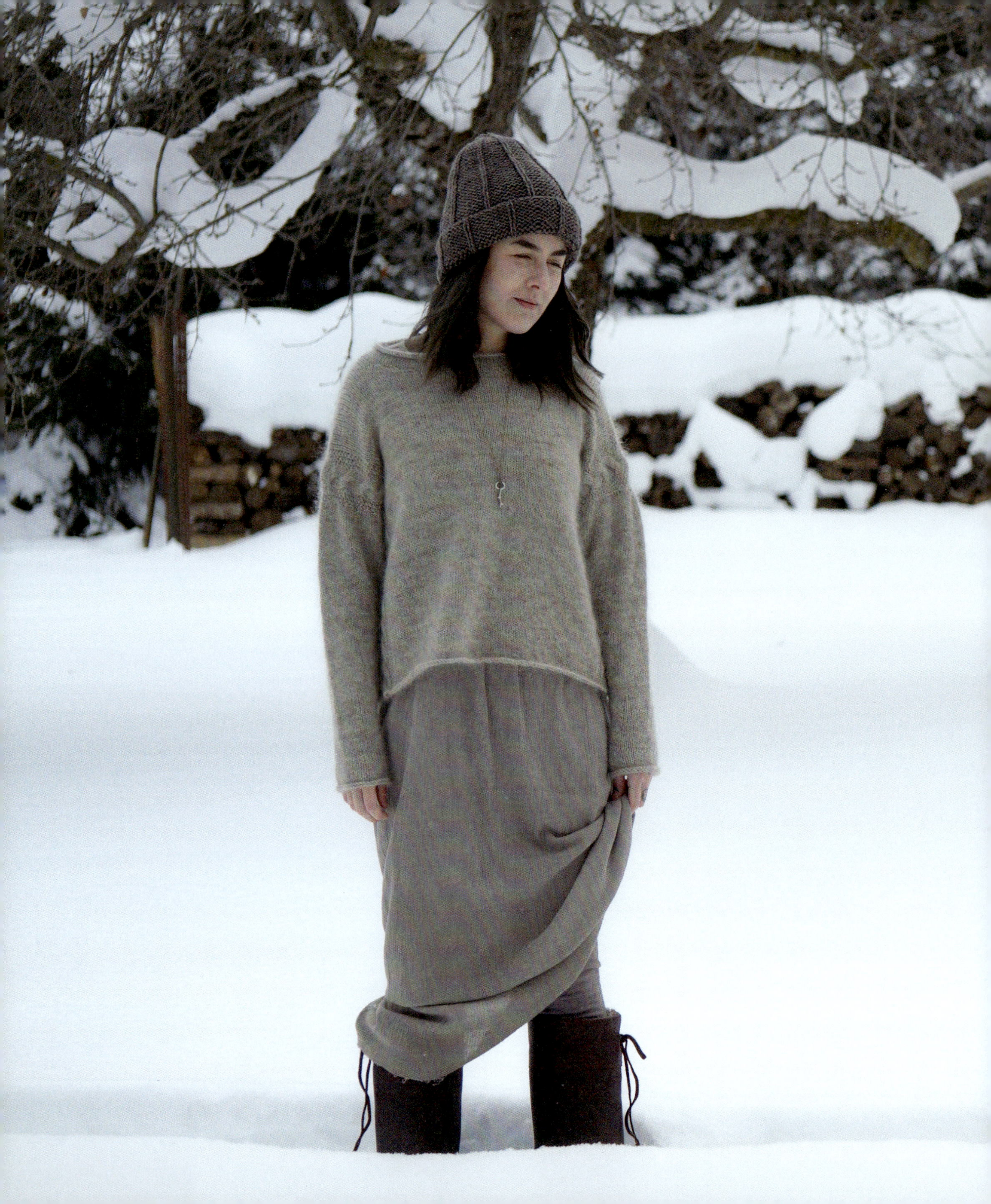

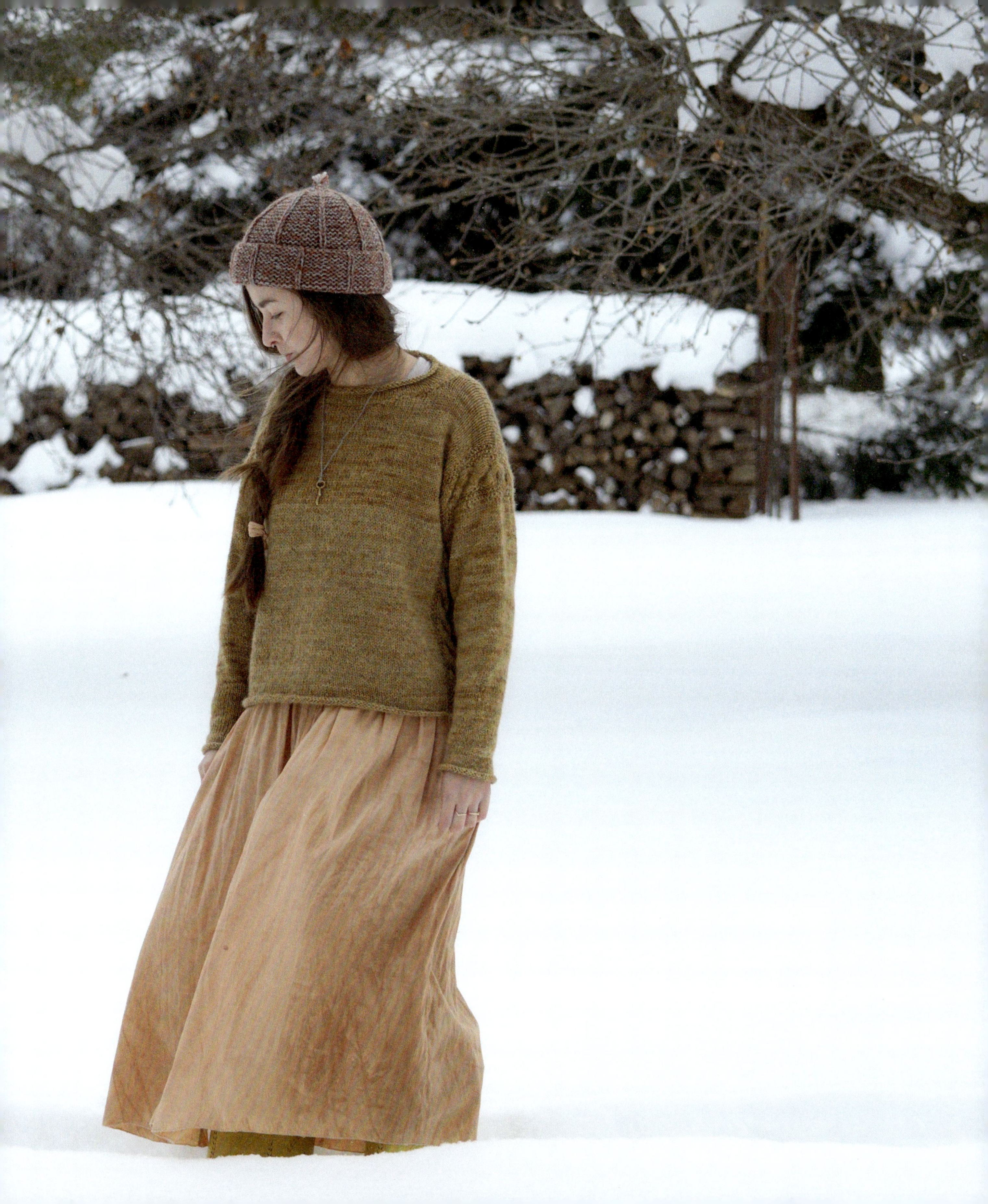

Soirée

Sizes: 1 (2, 3, 4, 5, 6, 7)
Finished bust circumference: 104 (116, 128, 139, 151, 162, 170) cm / 41 (45½, 50, 55, 59½, 64, 67)" - to be worn with 30-40 cm / 12-16" positive ease
Models have 84 cm / 33" bust, are both wearing sizes 2, with 32 cm / 13" positive ease.

PINK VERSION:
Yarn A: Viola Polwarth + Alpaca (3 ply / light fingering weight; 70% Polwarth wool, 15% white alpaca, 15% natural brown alpaca; 500 m / 547 yds per 100 g skein)
Shade: Giant Peach; 3 (3, 3, 4, 4, 4, 5) skeins
Yarn B: Viola Mohair Lace (lace weight; 72% mohair, 28% silk; 420 m / 459 yds per 50 g skein)
Shade: Rose Gold Dust; 3 (3, 4, 4, 4, 5, 5) skeins

GREY VERSION:
Yarn A: As for Original Version.
Shade: Garden Ghost
Yarn B: As for Original Version
Shade: Ghost

GOLDEN VERSION:
Yarn C: Viola Mooresburg DK (DK weight; 100% Cotswold/Dorset Wool; 283 m / 260 yds per 100 g skein)
Shade: Dirty Mustard; 4 (5, 5, 6, 7, 8, 8) skeins

Gauge: 21 sts & 30 rounds = 10 cm / 4" over St st in the round on 4.5 mm needles, with 1 strand each of yarns A and B held together, **OR** one strand of yarn C, after blocking

Needles: 4 mm / US 6 circular needle, 80 cm / 32" length AND needles suitable for working small circumferences in the round
4.5 mm / US 7 circular needle, 80 cm / 32" length AND needles suitable for working small circumferences in the round
Always use a needle size that will result in the correct gauge after blocking.

Notions: 8 stitch markers, cable needle, stitch holders or scrap yarn, blocking pins (optional, but useful to block out excess curl along bottom edge and neck of garment), tapestry needle.

Notes: Soirée is worked in the round, from the bottom cast-on edge to the underarms, then the front and back are knit flat separately from underarms to shoulders. Shoulder seams are grafted before picking up stitches around armholes and knitting the sleeves down to the cuffs. Sweater edges are intended to curl slightly, but are finished with a subtle cable to control the amount of curl. Hold one strand of yarn A and B together throughout **OR** one strand of yarn C **only** if working with a DK weight yarn, as per Golden Version. To adjust body length, add / remove complete repeats of Cable A only. It is important that all sizes end with pattern row 2 before grafting shoulders.

Stitch Glossary
4/4 LC: Slip 4 sts to cable needle, hold in front, k4, k4 from cable needle.
4/4 RC: Slip 4 sts to cable needle, hold in back, k4, k4 from cable needle.
LT: Insert needle into second st on LH needle, knit this st without slipping it off the needle. Knit first st on LH needle and slip both sts off needle.
RT: Slip 2 sts kwise, then slip them back to LH needle putting a twist into the second st (the first st being slipped back onto LH needle). Knit into back loop of second st on LH needle (this is the twisted st) without slipping it off the needle, knit first st and slip both sts off the needle.

CHARTS - WRITTEN INSTRUCTIONS
Chart A, worked in the round
(worked over 14 sts and 10 rounds)
Round 1: K1, p1, k1, 4/4 RC, k1, p1, k1.
Round 2: P1, k1, p1, k8, p1, k1, p1.
Round 3: K1, p1, k10, p1, k1.
Round 4: P1, k1, p1, k8, p1, k1, p1.
Rounds 5-10: Rep rounds 3-4.
Rep rounds 1-10 for pattern.

Chart A, worked flat in rows
(Worked over 14 sts and 10 rows)
Row 1 (RS): K1, p1, k1, 4/4 RC, k1, p1, k1.
Row 2 (WS): K1, p1, k1, p8, k1, p1, k1.
Row 3: K1, p1, k10, p1, k1.
Row 4: K1, p1, k1, p8, k1, p1, k1.
Rows 5-10: Rep rows 3-4.
Rep rows 1-10 for pattern.

Chart B, worked in the round
(Worked over 14 sts and 10 rounds)
Round 1: K1, p1, k1, 4/4 LC, k1, p1, k1.
Round 2: P1, k1, p1, k8, p1, k1, p1.
Round 3: K1, p1, k10, p1, k1.
Round 4: P1, k1, p1, k8, p1, k1, p1.
Rounds 5-10: Rep rounds 3-4.
Rep rounds 1-10 for pattern.

Chart B, worked flat in rows
(Worked over 14 sts and 10 rows)
Row 1 (RS): K1, p1, k1, 4/4 LC, k1, p1, k1.
Row 2 (WS): K1, p1, k1, p8, k1, p1, k1.
Row 3: K1, p1, k10, p1, k1.
Row 4: K1, p1, k1, p8, k1, p1, k1.
Rows 5-10: Rep rows 3-4.
Rep rows 1-10 for pattern.

Chart C, worked in the round
Round 1: RT, LT.
Round 2: Knit.
Round 3: LT, RT.
Round 4: Knit.
Rep rounds 1-4 for pattern.

PATTERN BEGINS

Note: Work with one strand of yarns A and B held together throughout **OR** one strand of yarn C **only** if working with a DK weight yarn, as per Golden Version.

BODY

Using smaller needle and long-tail method, cast on 216 (240, 264, 288, 312, 336, 352) sts. Join for working in the round being careful not to twist. PM to indicate beg of round.

Set-up round 1: *K1, p1, k1, k8, k1, p1, k1, PM, k64 (76, 88, 100, 108, 120, 128) sts, PM, k1, p1, k1, k8, k1, p1, k1, PM, k16 (16, 16, 16, 20, 20, 20), PM; rep from * once more noting that beg of round marker replaces last PM. *8 markers now placed*

Set-up round 2: *P1, k1, p1, k to 3 sts before next marker, p1, k1, p1, SM, k to next marker, SM, p1, k1, p1, k to 3 sts before next marker, p1, k1, p1, SM, k to next marker, SM; rep from * once more.

Commence cable patterns as foll:

Round 1: *Reading from Charts or Written Instructions, work round 1 of Chart A (in the round) across next 14 sts, SM, work Round 1 of Chart C to next marker, SM, work round 1 of Chart B (in the round) across next 14 sts, SM, work round 1 of Chart C to next marker, SM; rep from * once more.

Round 2: *Work round 2 of Chart A to next marker, SM, k to marker, SM, work round 2 of Chart B to next marker, SM, work round 2 of Chart C as set to next marker, SM; rep from * once more.

Change to larger needle.

Round 3: *Work next round of Chart A to marker, k to marker, work next round of Chart B to next marker, SM, work next round of Chart C as set to next marker, SM; rep from * once more.

Continue as set by round 3, working reps of Charts A, B and C until a total of 7 (7, 7, 7, 8, 8, 8) reps of Chart A have been worked then work a further 3 (3, 7, 7, 1, 9, 3) rounds.

Divide for Front and Back:

*Work next row of Chart A, SM, k to next marker, SM, work next row of Chart B, work across 16 (16, 16, 16, 20, 20, 20) Chart C sts, then slip these 16 (16, 16, 16, 20, 20, 20) Chart C sts onto stitch holder or scrap yarn for underarm. Remove markers on either side of Chart C sts; rep from * once more. Do not break yarn. *92 (104, 116, 128, 136, 148, 156) sts each Front and Back*

Front and Back pieces are now worked separately back and forth in rows – follow instructions for Charts A and B for working flat in rows. 1 stitch will be cast on at beg and end of row to form a selvedge stitch for use later when picking up sleeve sts. Work selvedge sts in St st throughout.

BACK

Set-up row (RS): Using the cable cast on method, cast 1 st onto LH needle for selvedge st, knit this st, work next row of Chart A, SM, k to next marker, SM, work next row of Chart B, turn work. *93 (105, 117, 129, 137, 149, 157) sts*

Set-up row (WS): Using the cable cast on method, cast 1 st onto LH needle for selvedge st, purl this st, work next row of Chart B, SM, p to next marker, SM, work next row of Chart A, p1. *94 (106, 118, 130, 138, 150, 158) sts*

Continue as foll:

Row 1 (RS): K1, work next row of Chart A, SM, k to next marker, SM, work next row of Chart B, k1.

Row 2 (WS): P1, work next row of Chart B, SM, p to next marker, SM, work next row of Chart A, p1.

Last 2 rows set patt.

Continue as set until a total of 13 (13, 13, 14, 14, 15, 16) reps of Chart A have been completed from cast-on edge then work 2 more rows, ending with a WS row and row 2 of Chart A.

Place first 27 (31, 36, 41, 44, 49, 52) sts on stitch holder or scrap yarn for left shoulder, cast off next 40 (44, 46, 48, 50, 52, 54) sts, place rem 27 (31, 36, 41, 44, 49, 52) sts on stitch holder or scrap yarn for right shoulder.

FRONT

With RS facing, rejoin yarn at left front underarm. Follow instructions for Back until a total of 11 (11, 11, 12, 11, 12, 13) Chart A reps have been completed from cast-on edge then work a further 4 (4, 2, 0, 8, 8, 6) rows.

Divide for Left and Right Front (RS): K1, work Chart A, SM, k26 (31, 36, 42, 45, 51, 55) sts, cast off next 12 (14, 16, 16, 18, 18, 18) sts, k26 (31, 36, 42, 45, 51, 55) sts, work Chart B, k1. *82 (92, 102, 114, 120, 132, 140) sts; 41 (46, 51, 57, 60, 66, 70) sts each side of neck*

Right and Left Fronts are now worked separately as foll:

RIGHT FRONT

Next row (WS and all foll WS rows): P1, work Chart B, SM, p to end.

Working WS rows as set and maintaining Chart B, cast off 5 sts at beg of next RS row, 3 sts at beg of next 2 (3, 3, 3, 3, 4, 4) RS rows, 2 sts at beg of next 1 (0, 0, 1, 1, 0, 0) RS row and 1 st at beg of next 1 (1, 1, 0, 0, 0, 1) RS rows. *27 (31, 36, 41, 44, 49, 52) sts*

Work 7 (7, 9, 11, 13, 13, 13) rows straight, ending with a WS Row 2 of Chart B.

Place rem 27 (31, 36, 41, 44, 49, 52) sts on stitch holder or scrap yarn.

LEFT FRONT

With WS facing, rejoin yarn to Left Front sts.

Next row (WS): P to marker, SM, work Chart A, p1.

Next row (RS and all following RS rows): K1, work Chart A, SM, k to end.

Working RS rows as set and maintaining Chart A, cast off 5 sts at beg of next WS row, 3 sts at beg of next 2 (3, 3, 3, 3, 4, 4) WS rows, 2 sts at

Soirée

beg of next 1 (0, 0, 1, 1, 0, 0) WS rows and 1 st at beg of next 1 (1, 1, 0, 0, 0, 1) WS rows. *27 (31, 36, 41, 44, 49, 52) sts*
Work 6 (6, 8, 10, 12, 12, 12) rows straight, ending with a WS row 2 of Chart A.
Place rem 27 (31, 36, 41, 44, 49, 52) sts on stitch holder or scrap yarn.
Graft shoulder seams together using Kitchener stitch.

SLEEVES (both alike)
Slip 16 (16, 16, 16, 20, 20, 20) Chart C sts from holder onto larger needle suitable for small circumferences, PM, pick up and k30 (33, 37, 37, 39, 46, 46) sts from underarm to shoulder seam, then 30 (33, 37, 37, 39, 46, 46) sts from shoulder seam to underarm. Join for working in the round and PM to indicate beg of round. *76 (82, 90, 90, 98, 112, 112) sts*

Next round: Work Chart C as set, SM, k to end of round.
Last round sets Sleeve patt.
Work 1 round in patt.
Next round (Dec): Work Chart C as set, SM, k2, k2tog, k to 4 sts before end of round, ssk, k2. *2 sts dec*
Continue in patt as set and rep Dec round every 3rd round 0 (0, 2, 2, 6, 30, 19) times, every 4th round 0 (4, 16, 16, 16, 1, 5) times, every 5th round 4 (14, 4, 4, 2, 0, 5) times, then every 6th round 11 (0, 0, 0, 0, 0, 0) times. *44 (44, 44, 44, 48, 48, 52) sts*
Work straight in patt until Sleeve measures 34 (34, 35.5, 35.5, 37, 37, 40.5) cm / 13½ (13½, 14, 14, 14½, 14½, 16)" from pick-up ending with round 1 or 3 of Chart C.

Change to smaller needle suitable for small circumferences.
Next round: Work Chart C to marker, SM, k to end.
Next round: Rep next row of Chart C (row 1 or 3) 11 (11, 11, 11, 12, 12, 13) times across the round.
Next 2 rounds: Knit.
Cast off loosely using larger needle if required.

FINISHING
Weave in ends and block to measurements. You may want to pin the cast-on edge down to prevent it rolling back.
NECKBAND
With RS facing, using smaller needle suitable for small circumferences, pick up and k40 (44, 46, 48, 50, 52, 54) Back neck sts, PM, pick up and k21 (22, 24, 27, 29, 30, 31) sts along left neck, 12 (14, 16, 16, 18, 18, 18) sts in centre front cast off, 21 (22, 24, 27, 29, 30, 31) sts along right neck. Join for working in the round and PM to indicate beg of round. *94 (102, 110, 118, 126, 130, 134) sts*
Round 1: Knit.
Round 2: K2, k2tog, k to 4 sts before marker, ssk, k2, SM, k to end.
2 sts dec
Rounds 3-4: Knit.
Rep rounds 2-4 twice more. *88 (96, 104, 112, 120, 124, 128) sts*
Next round: Rep row 1 of Chart C 22 (24, 26, 28, 30, 31, 32) times across the round.
Next round: Knit.
Cast off loosely using larger needle if required.

CHART A – worked both in the round and flat in rows

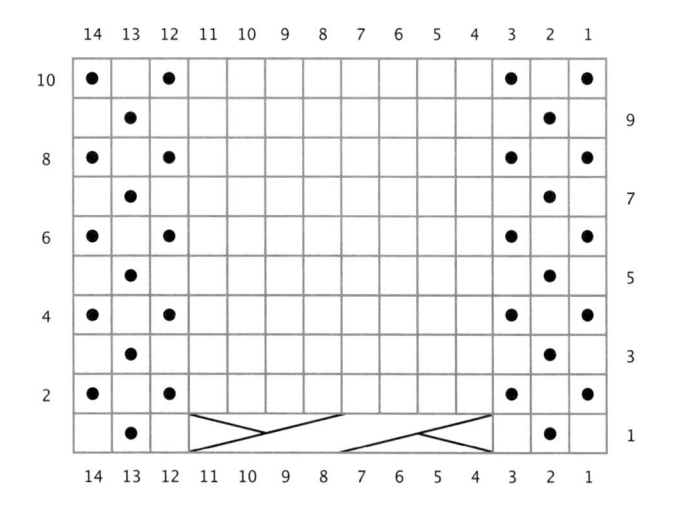

CHART B – worked both in the round and flat in rows

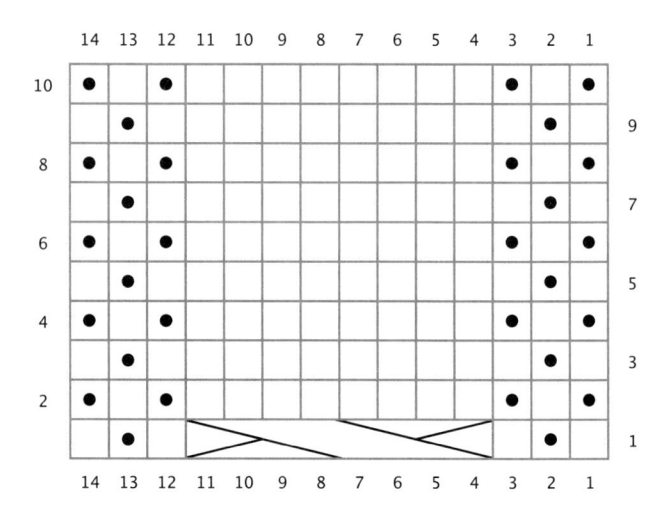

CHART C

Key

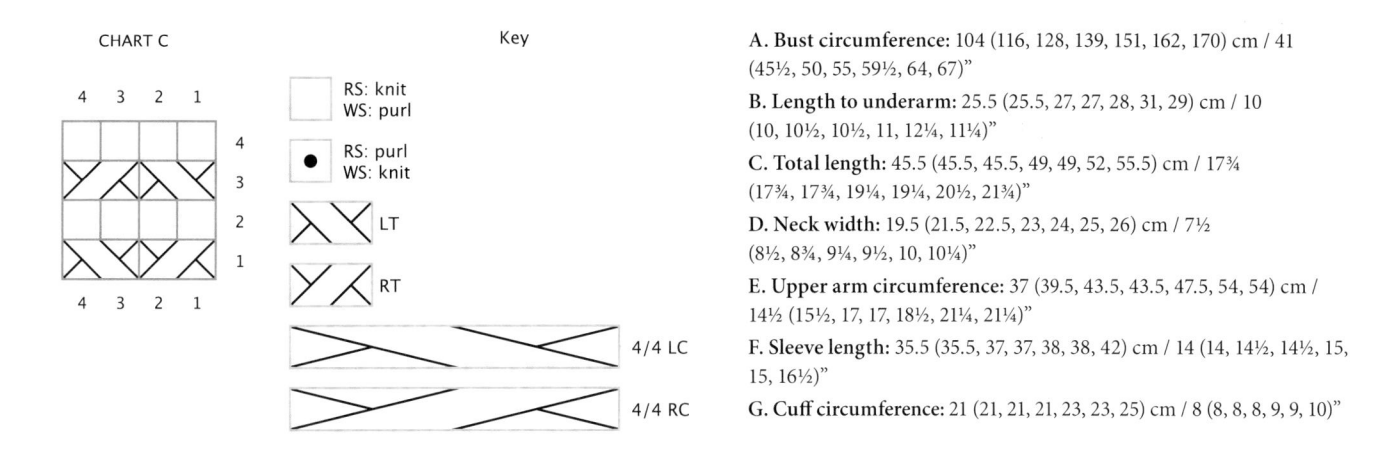

- RS: knit / WS: purl
- RS: purl / WS: knit
- LT
- RT
- 4/4 LC
- 4/4 RC

A. Bust circumference: 104 (116, 128, 139, 151, 162, 170) cm / 41 (45½, 50, 55, 59½, 64, 67)"

B. Length to underarm: 25.5 (25.5, 27, 27, 28, 31, 29) cm / 10 (10, 10½, 10½, 11, 12¼, 11¼)"

C. Total length: 45.5 (45.5, 45.5, 49, 49, 52, 55.5) cm / 17¾ (17¾, 17¾, 19¼, 19¼, 20½, 21¾)"

D. Neck width: 19.5 (21.5, 22.5, 23, 24, 25, 26) cm / 7½ (8½, 8¾, 9¼, 9½, 10, 10¼)"

E. Upper arm circumference: 37 (39.5, 43.5, 43.5, 47.5, 54, 54) cm / 14½ (15½, 17, 17, 18½, 21¼, 21¼)"

F. Sleeve length: 35.5 (35.5, 37, 37, 38, 38, 42) cm / 14 (14, 14½, 14½, 15, 15, 16½)"

G. Cuff circumference: 21 (21, 21, 21, 23, 23, 25) cm / 8 (8, 8, 8, 9, 9, 10)"

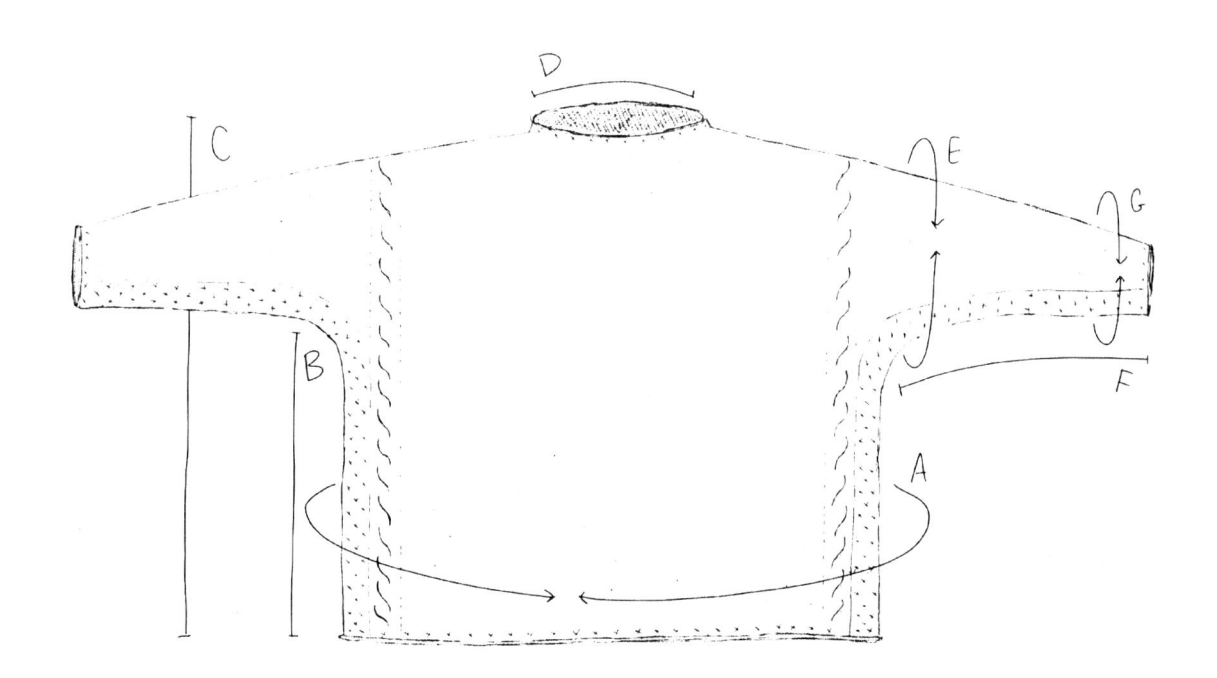

93

94

Winter Berry

Winterberry is all about the simple textures that jump off a smooth, snow-covered background. Only a tiny portion of buried vegetation pokes out of deep snow, interrupting its white surface. Scruffy little clusters of shrubs and bent-over blades of grass dot expansive, white fields like little islands of texture. Upon closer inspection, these texture islands are full of colour and pattern too, with an occasional bittersweet berry appearing in their tangles of brown. Its colour is all the brighter because it is such a surprise to see. I have included an option to knit some of the bobbles on this vest in a contrasting yarn, giving the knitter the option to choose their placement. Just as those little texture islands and hidden berries of the winter landscape seem to appear at random, you can place your contrasting bobbles in any pattern (or non-pattern) you like!

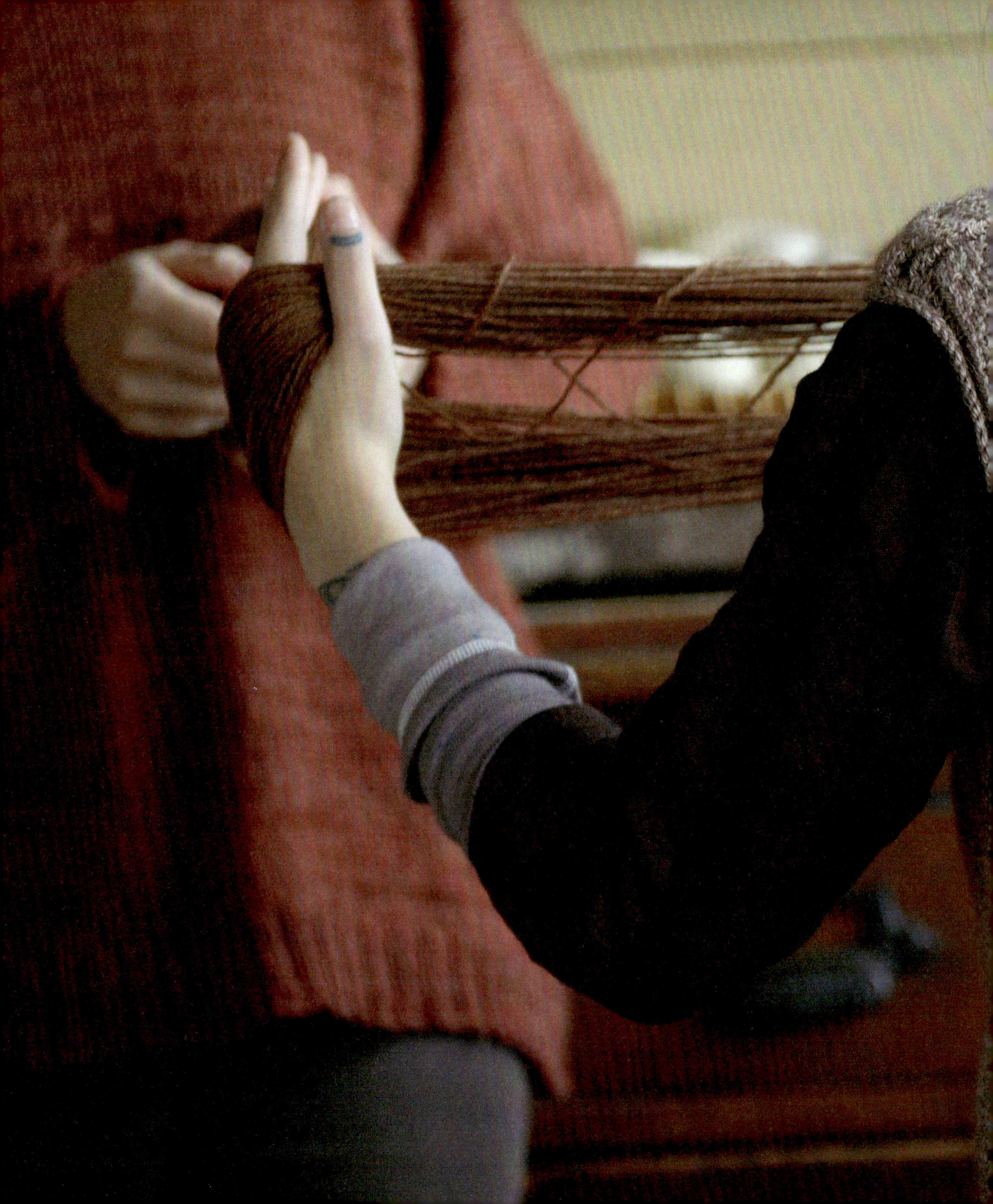

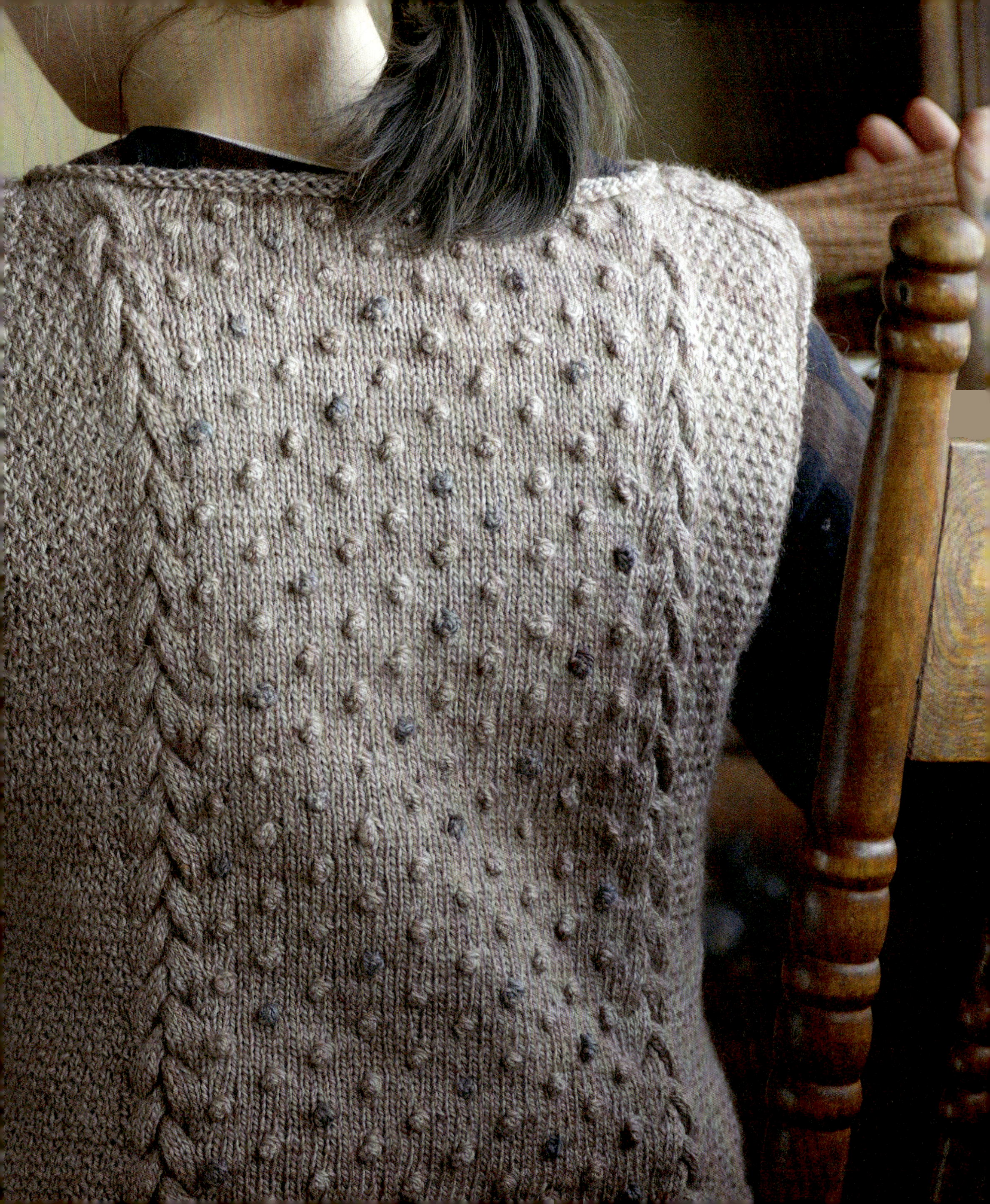

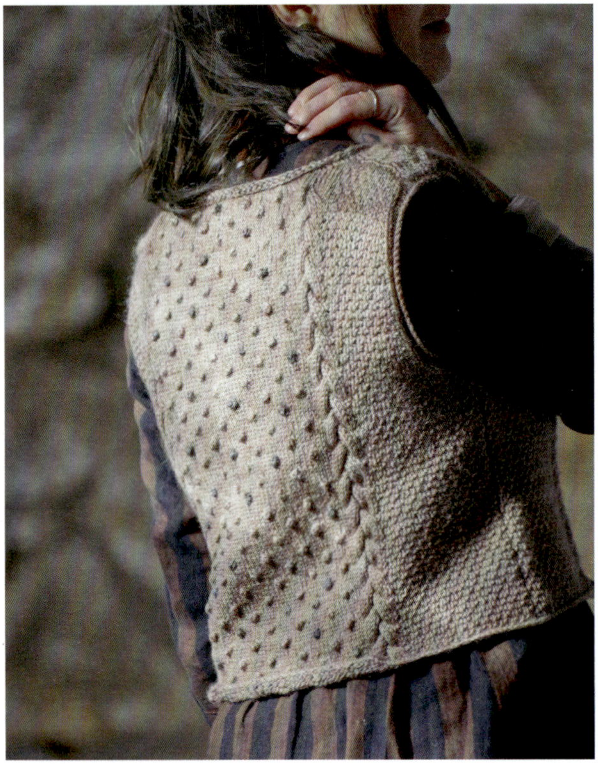

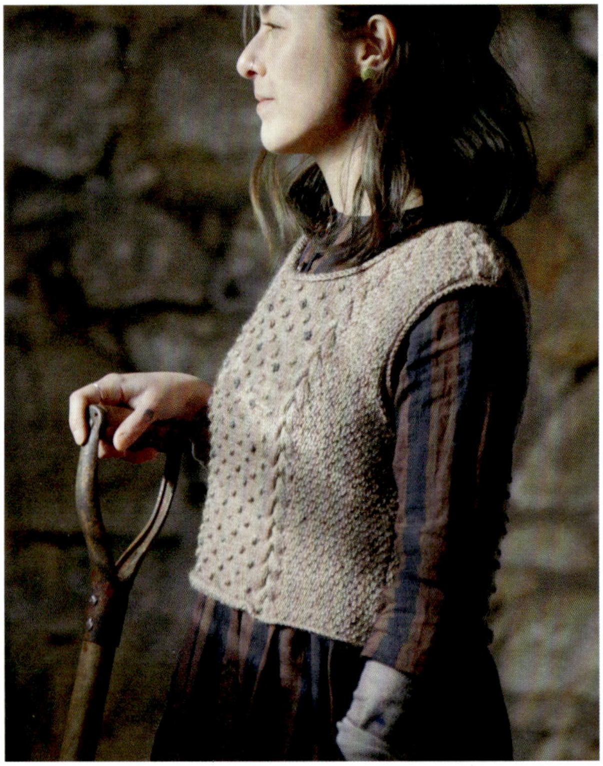

Sizes: 1 (2, 3, 4, 5, 6)
Finished bust circumference: 86.5 (92.5, 99.5, 110, 120, 130) cm / 34 (36½, 39¼, 43¼, 47¼, 51¼)" – to be worn with approx. 2.5-7.5 cm / 1-3" positive ease
Model has 84 cm / 33" bust, is wearing a size 1, with 2.5 cm / 1" positive ease.
Yarn: Viola Mooresburg DK (DK weight; 100% Cotswold/Dorset Wool; 238 m / 260 yds per 100 g skein)
Shades:
Yarn A: Asteroid: 3 (3, 4, 4, 5, 5) skeins
Yarn B: Mooresburg: 1 skein
Gauge: 22.5 sts & 31 rounds = 10 cm / 4" over Bobble Panel pattern in the round on 4 mm needles, after blocking
24 sts & 28 rounds = 10 cm / 4" over Double Seed Stitch in the round on 4 mm needles, after blocking
12 sts of Cable A/B = 2.5 cm / 1" wide
Needles: 4 mm / US 6 circular needle, 80 cm / 32" length, for working body in the round and flat **AND** knitting needles suitable for working small circumferences in the round
Always use a needle size that will result in the correct gauge after blocking.
Notions: Cable needle, 10 stitch markers, stitch holders or scrap yarn, tapestry needle
Notes: Winterberry Vest is knit from the bottom up in one piece. It is worked in the round to the underarms, then the front and back are knit flat to form armholes. A purled faux seam runs up the right and left side body to underarms. Panels of bobble stitches and cables run up the centre back and front. Some bobbles are worked in short lengths of contrasting yarn. Front shoulder stitches are finished with a cabled knit bind off, which is then seamed to the back shoulder stitches.
When working contrasting bobbles, use a pre-cut length of yarn, approx. 30 cm / 12" long. Sample shown with one bobble per Rows 1 & 5 worked in contrasting yarn.

Stitch Glossary
4/4 RC: Slip 4 sts to cable needle, hold at front, k4, k4 from cable needle.
4/4 LC: Slip 4 sts to cable needle, hold at back, k4, k4 from cable needle.

MB (Make Bobble):
Note: When working contrasting bobbles, work rows 1 & 2 in yarn B and row 3 in yarn A.
Row 1 (RS): Kfbf, turn.
Row 2 (WS): P3, turn.
Row 3 (RS): S2kpo.

Double Seed Stitch, worked in the round
(Worked over a multiple of 2 sts + 1 and 4 rounds)
Rounds 1-2: [K1, p1] to last st, k1.
Rounds 3-4: [P1, k1] to last st, p1.
Rep rounds 1-4 for pattern.

Double Seed Stitch, worked flat in rows
(Worked over a multiple of 2 sts + 1 and 4 rounds)
Row 1 (RS): [K1, p1] to last st, k1.
Row 2 (WS): [P1, k1] to last st, p1.
Row 3: Rep row 2.
Row 4: Rep row 1.
Rep rows 1-4 for pattern.

Cable A, worked in the round
(Worked over 12 sts and 12 rounds)
Round 1: K4, 4/4 RC.
Rounds 2-6: Knit.
Round 7: 4/4 LC, k4.
Rounds 8-11: Knit.
Round 12: Knit.
Rep rounds 1-12 for pattern.

Cable A, worked flat in rows
(Worked over 12 sts and 12 rows)
Row 1 (RS): K4, 4/4 RC.
Row 2 and all WS rows: Purl.
Rows 3 & 5: Knit.
Row 7: 4/4 LC, k4.
Rows 8-11: Rep rows 2-5.
Row 12 (WS): Purl.
Rep rows 1-12 for pattern.

Cable B, worked in the round
(Worked over 12 sts and 12 rounds)
Round 1: 4/4 LC, k4.
Rounds 2-6: Knit.
Round 7: K4, 4/4 RC.
Rounds 8-11: Knit.
Round 12: Knit.
Rep rounds 1-12 for pattern.

Cable B, worked flat in rows
(Worked over 12 sts and 12 rows)
Row 1: 4/4 LC, k4.
Row 2 and all WS rows: Purl.
Rows 3 & 5: Knit.

Winterberry

Row 7: K4, 4/4 RC.
Rows 8-11: Rep rows 2-5.
Row 12: Purl.
Rep rows 1-12 for pattern.

Bobble Panel, worked flat in rows
(Worked over a multiple of 8 sts and 8 rows)
Note: Work 1 bobble in rows 1 & 5 in yarn B (see Pattern Notes) and the rest in yarn A.
Row 1 (RS): [K2, MB, k5] to end.
Row 2 (and all WS rows): Purl.
Row 3: Knit.
Row 5 (RS): [K6, MB, k1] to end.
Row 7: Knit.
Row 8 (WS): Purl.
Rep rows 1-8 for pattern.

Bobble Panel, worked in the round
(Worked over a multiple of 8 sts and 8 rounds)
Note: Work 1 bobble in rounds 1 & 5 in yarn B (see Pattern Notes) and the rest in yarn A.
Round 1: [K2, MB, k5] to end.
Rounds 2-4: Knit.
Round 5: [K6, MB, k1] to end.
Rounds 6-8: Knit.
Rep rounds 1-8 for pattern.

PATTERN BEGINS
BODY
Using circular needle, yarn A, and long-tail method, cast on 222 (238, 254, 278, 302, 326) sts.
Join for working in the round, being careful not to twist sts. PM to indicate beg of round.

Edging
Round 1: Knit.
Round 2: [K1 with A, k1 with B]. Break yarn B.
Round 3: Rep round 1.

Set-up Round: [P1, PM, work Double Seed Stitch over next 23 (27, 31, 37, 43, 49) sts, PM, work Cable A over next 12 sts, PM, work Bobble Panel over centre 40 sts, PM, work Cable B over next 12 sts, PM, work Double Seed Stitch over next 23 (27, 31, 37, 43, 49) sts, PM] twice.
Next Round: [P1, SM, work Double Seed Stitch to next marker, SM, work Cable A, SM, work Bobble Panel, SM, work Cable B, SM, work Double Seed to next marker, SM] twice.

Continue in pattern as set, working the next round of Bobble Panel, Double Seed and Cable patterns A & B each time, until work measures 24 cm / 9½" or desired length for body.

Shape Armholes
Next round: Work 107 (115, 122, 133, 144, 155) sts in patt, cast off 9 (9, 11, 13, 15, 17) sts removing marker as you pass it, work 102 (110, 116, 126, 136, 146) sts in patt, cast off 9 (9, 11, 13, 15, 17) sts, removing beg of round marker as you pass it. *102 (110, 116, 126, 136, 146) sts each for front and back*
Slip Back sts to holder while working Upper Front. Piece is now worked flat to shape armholes.

UPPER FRONT
Row 1 (RS): K1 (**Note:** on first rep this has already been worked as part of armhole cast-off), k2tog, patt to last 3 sts of Front, ssk, k1. *2 sts dec*
Row 2 (WS): P2, patt to last 2 sts, p2.
Rep rows 1-2 a further 3 (5, 6, 8, 10, 11) times. *94 (98, 102, 108, 114, 122) sts*
Continue in patt as set, working 2 selvedge sts at beg and end of row in St st, until Upper Front measures 10 (12.5, 15, 16.5, 18, 19) cm / 4 (5, 6, 6½, 7, 7½)" from first armhole cast-off row, ending with a WS row.

Shape Neck
Bobble Panel sts are now cast off to shape neck, over the next 7.5 cm / 3". Cables A & B remain on either side of neck opening.
Next row (RS): Patt to end of Cable A, SM, k12, cast off next 16 sts, k to marker, SM, patt to end. *39 (41, 43, 46, 49, 53) sts on either side of neck; 78 (82, 86, 92, 98, 106) total Front sts*
Continue on Right Front sts only; place Left Front sts on holder or scrap yarn.

Right Front
Working in patt as est throughout, cast off 3 sts at beg of next 3 RS rows, then 2 sts at beg of foll RS row. *28 (30, 32, 35, 38, 42) sts*
Continue straight in patt until Right Front measures 18 (20.5, 23, 24, 25.5, 26.5) cm / 7 (8, 9, 9½, 10, 10½)" from first armhole cast-off row, ending with a WS row.

Next Row (RS): Using cable cast-on method, cast on 2 selvedge sts, sl1 wyif, k1, work across Cable B pattern as set, cast on 1 selvedge st using cable method, turn.
Next Row (WS): Sl1 wyif, patt to last 2 sts, p1, k1.
The cable will now be knit perpendicularly onto live Right Front sts as follows:
Row 1 (RS): Sl1 wyif, k1, patt to last st, ssk (1 st from previous row

with 1 Right Front shoulder st), turn.
Row 2 (WS): Sl1 wyif, patt to last 2 sts, p1, k1.
Rep rows 1-2 until all 15 (17, 19, 22, 25, 29) Double Seed sts have been incorporated into the cable. Cast off rem 16 sts.

Left Front
With RS facing, rejoin yarn to held Left Front sts. *39 (41, 43, 46, 49, 53) sts*
Working in patt as est throughout, cast off 3 sts at beg of next 3 WS rows, then 2 sts at beg of foll WS row. *28 (30, 32, 35, 38, 42) sts*
Continue straight in patt until work measures 18 (20.5, 23, 24, 25.5, 26.5) cm / 7 (8, 9, 9½, 10, 10½)" from first armhole cast-off row, ending with a WS row.

Next row (RS): Work across Double Seed sts to marker, remove marker, using cable cast-on method, cast on 1 st, k this st, patt to end.
Next Row (WS): Using cable cast-on method, cast on 2 sts, sl1 wyif, p1, patt to last 2 sts, p1, k1.
The cable will now be knit perpendicularly onto live Left Front sts as follows:
Row 1 (RS): Patt to end.
Row 2 (WS): Sl1 wyif, patt across Cable A sts, p2tog (1 st from previous row with 1 Left Front shoulder st), turn.
Rep rows 1-2 until all 15 (17, 19, 22, 25, 29) Double Seed sts have been incorporated into the cable. Cast off rem 16 sts.

BACK
Back Armhole Shaping
Return to 102 (110, 116, 126, 136, 146) held sts for Back. Rejoin yarn with RS facing.
Row 1 (RS): K1, k2tog, patt to last 3 sts, ssk, k1. *2 sts dec*
Row 2 (WS): P2, patt to last 2 sts, p2.
Repeat rows 1-2 a further 3 (5, 6, 8, 10, 11) times. *94 (98, 102, 108, 114, 122) sts*
Continue in set pattern until work measures 19 (21.5, 24, 25.5, 26.5, 28) cm / 7½ (8½, 9½, 10, 10½, 11)" from cast-on edge. Cast off all sts.

FINISHING
Sew selvedge edge of front cabled bands to bound off sts for back using mattress stitch.

Neckband
With RS facing, beg at right shoulder seam, using yarn A and needles suitable for knitting small circumferences in the round, pick up and knit 80 sts around neck opening. PM to indicate beg of round.
Round 1: With yarn A, knit.
Round 2: [K1 with yarn A, k1 with yarn B] to end.
Round 3: Rep round 1.
Cast off all sts with yarn A.

Armhole edgings
With RS facing, beg at centre of underarm, using yarn A and needles suitable for knitting small circumferences in the round, pick up and knit approx. 80 (90, 96, 100, 106, 112) sts around right armhole. PM to indicate beg of round. Work edging as for Neckband. Rep for left armhole.
Contrasting bobbles (if worked) will leave many ends inside garment. Gently knot ends and trim rather than weaving in, as contrasting yarn may show through on RS.
Weave in all remaining ends and block garment to measurements.

A. Bust circumference: 86.5 (92.5, 99.5, 110, 120, 130) cm / 34 (36½, 39¼, 43¼, 47¼, 51¼)"
B. Body length to underarm: 24 cm / 9½"
C. Front length to shoulder: 42 (44.5, 47, 48.5, 49.5, 51) cm / 16½ (17½, 18½, 19, 19½, 20)"
D. Front Armhole depth: 20.5 (23, 25.5, 26.5, 28, 29) cm / 8 (9, 10, 10½, 11, 11½)"
E. Back Armhole depth: 19 (21.5, 24, 25.5, 26.5, 28) cm / 7½ (8½, 9½, 10, 10½, 11)"

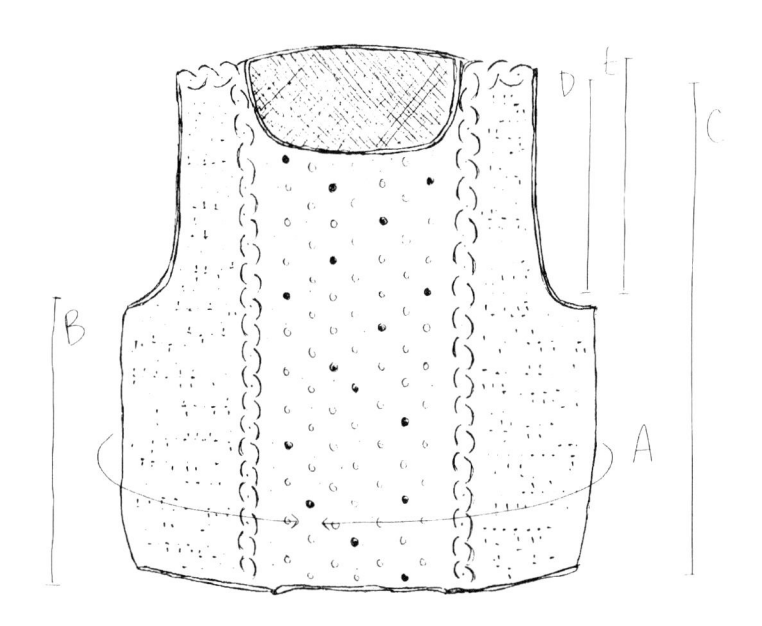

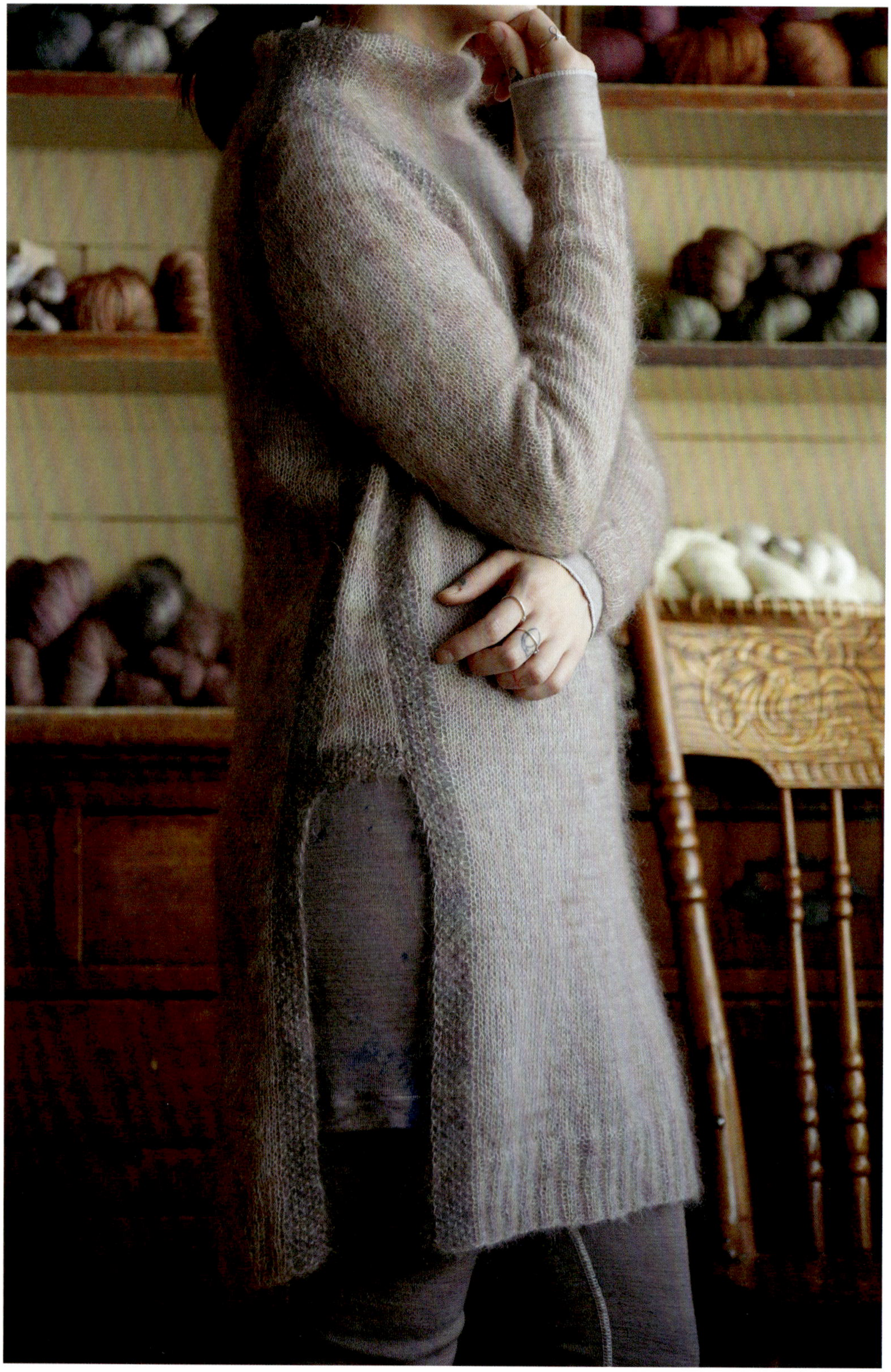

Frost is intended to be a warm, lightweight base layer that allows the wearer to move freely and explore the winter landscape. It is inspired by many long hours of gazing at frosty leaf skeletons in the dead of winter, wondering how their delicate forms have held up against the elements. I find it remarkable that these tough little things survive the wind, rain and weight of snow. Their transparent outlines persevere somehow. Just like these leaf skeletons, the Frost Tunic is surprisingly stronger and warmer than it looks. Don't let its delicate form fool you!

I use a technique in this pattern that has been referred to in the past as Blended Intarsia. While knitters have been working with this technique for years, the idea first occured to me after I knit the Humboldt Sweater by Anna Maltz. I was instantly inspired by the simplicity of Anna's Marlisle technique and the endless possibilities that it provided. Since the Humboldt sweater, Anna has gone on to write an entire book on the technique.

Marlisle: a New Direction in Knitting is a thorough and well-researched collection of patterns and information. I recommend that anyone seeking more information and background on Marlisle should read her book!

Anna's Marlisle combines marl knitting with Fair Isle, allowing two colours to be knit together (marled) or one at a time (Fair Isle). Frost uses a combination of marl knitting and Intarsia, which is very similar but not identical. I have used the term 'Blended Intarsia' here to avoid any confusion between Fair Isle and Intarsia.

Whatever you wish to call the technique used in this pattern, it was inspired by Anna and her Marlisle explorations.

The vertical stripes that run along the seam edges of the body, raglan and sleeves are knit holding two strands of yarn together while the centre body stitches are knit with just one of those strands, thus combining marl knitting with intarsia, rather than Fair Isle. The vertical lines running up the edges of each body piece are referred to as Decorative Raglan Seams (DRS), using Anna's terminology. Read on for the technical scoop.

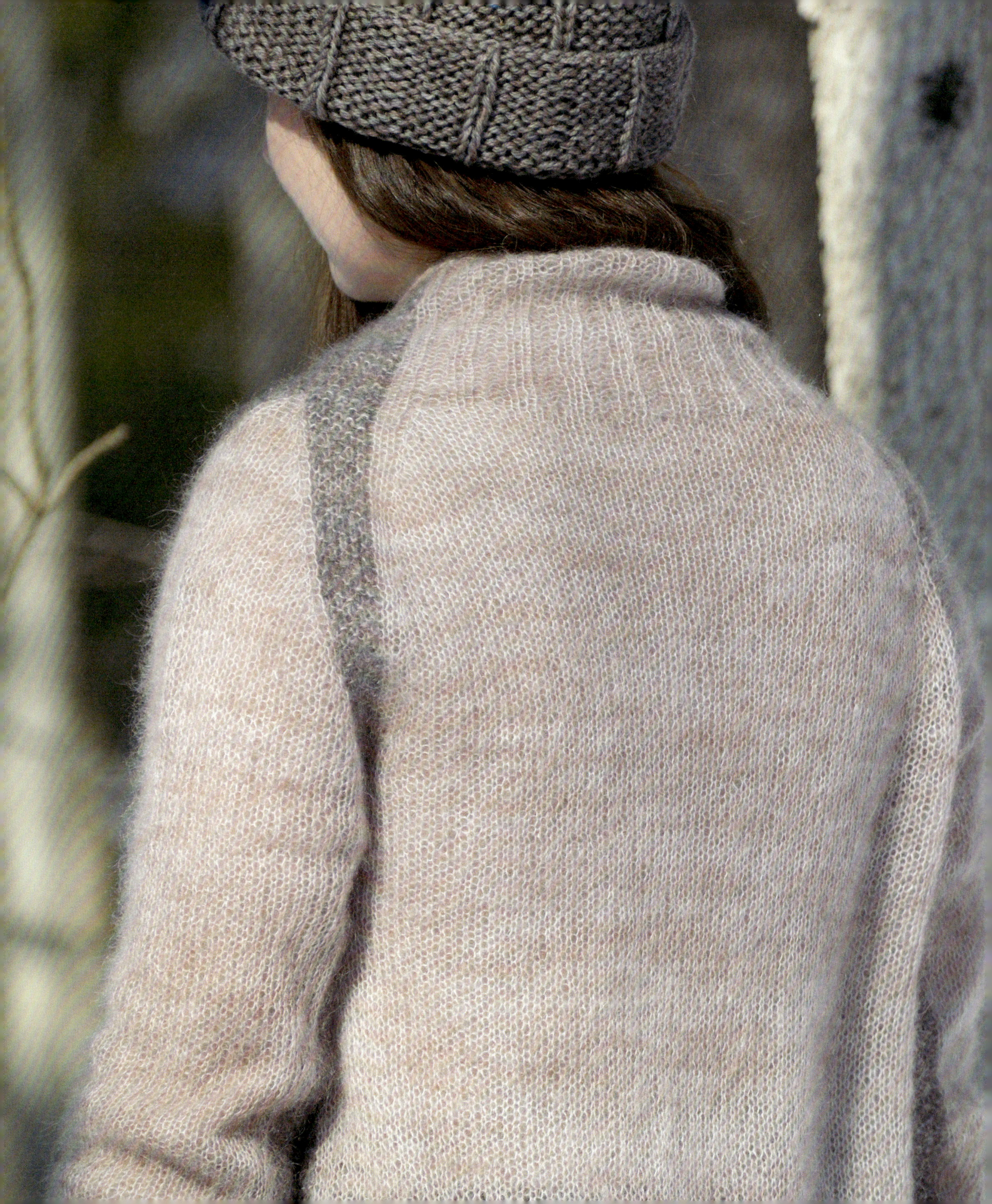

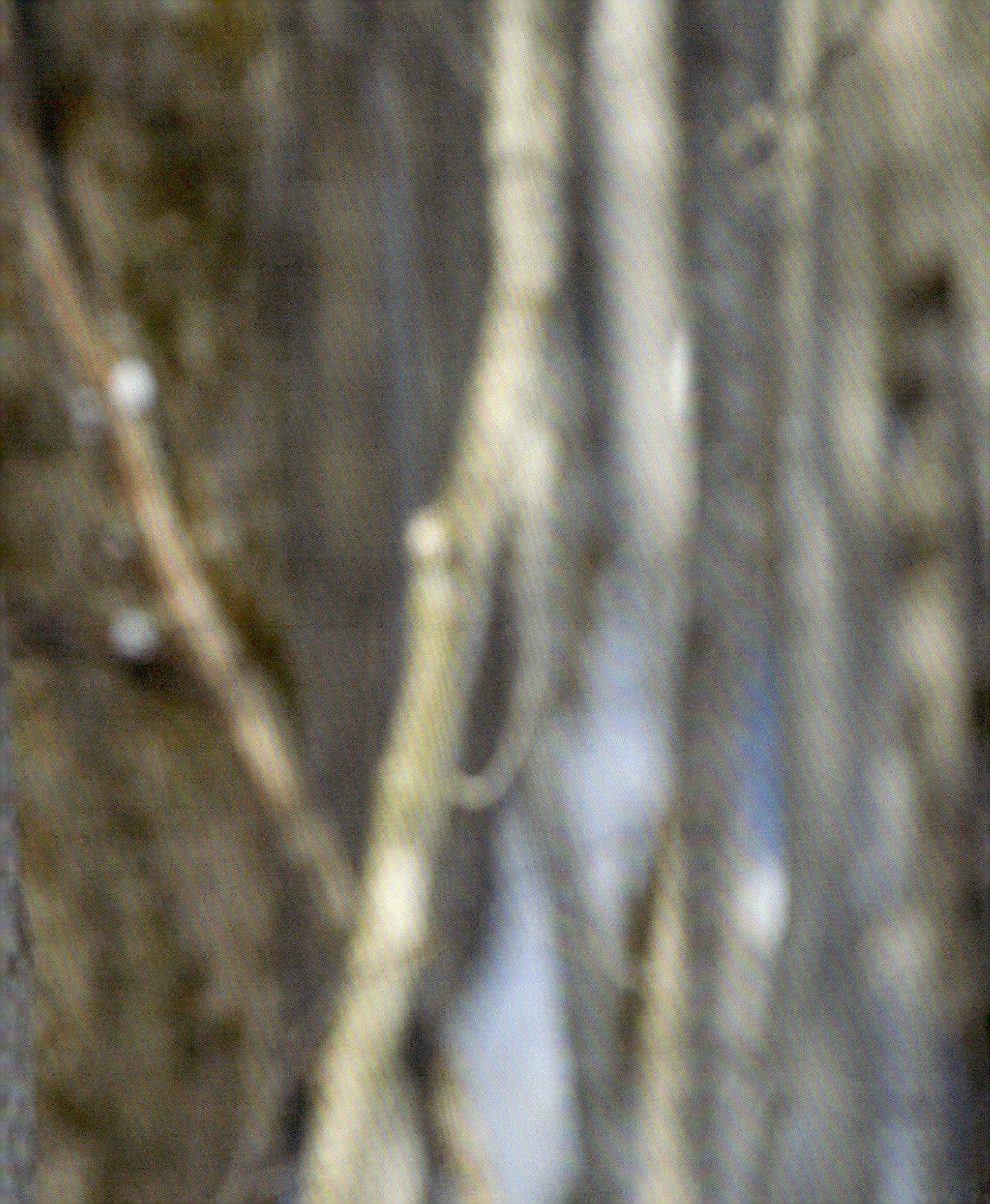

Frost

Sizes: 1 (2, 3, 4, 5, 6)
Finished bust circumference: 93.5 (101.5, 109, 117.5, 125.5, 133.5) cm / 36¾ (40, 43, 46¼, 49½, 52½)" – to be worn with 3-10 cm / 1-4" positive ease
Model has 84 cm / 33" bust, is wearing size 1 of the long version, with 9.5 cm / 3¾" positive ease.
Yarn: Viola Mohair Lace (lace weight; 72% kid mohair, 28% silk; 420 m / 459 yds per 50 g skein)
Shades:
Yarn A: Cygnet; 3 (3, 3, 3, 4, 4) skeins
Yarn B: Frozen Earth; 1 skein
Gauge: 20 sts & 28 rows = 10 cm / 4" over St st on 4 mm needles, after blocking
Needles: 4 mm / US 6 circular needle, 80 cm / 32" length
Always use a needle size that will result in the correct gauge after blocking.
Notions: 2 knitting bobbins for working Intarsia, 4 stitch markers, 2 split ring markers, tapestry needle
Notes: About 'Blended Intarsia': Decorative Raglan Seams (DRS) are formed by doubling yarn B with yarn A, while the remainder of work is knit with yarn A only. At points in knitting where yarn B is dropped and work continues in yarn A only, yarns can become twisted. Minimise twisting by separating yarns A and B with your ring finger when marling. A couple of little twists can be knit in and won't show up in finished work. Experiment with this while swatching. Knitting bobbins are recommended for holding yarn B. Frost Tunic is knit in pieces from the bottom up. Both long and short versions feature a triangular notch that is knit while working the back. The front neck is shaped with short rows and the collar is worked while knitting the body pieces. When casting on with this yarn, you may prefer to cast on using a larger needle (about twice the size of the gauge-size needle, or 2 pattern needles held together). This creates a sufficiently elastic cast-on edge.

Stitch Glossary
Seed Stitch
(worked over an even number of sts)
Row 1: [K1, p1] to end.
Row 2: Work sts opposite to how they appear (purling knit sts and knitting purl sts).
Rep row 2 for pattern.

Blended Intarsia:
DRS (Decorative Raglan Seam): Unless pattern states otherwise, the first and last 6 sts of every row are worked in Seed Stitch holding yarns A and B together. These sts are referred to as DRS.

Row 1 establishes this pattern and recommends the use of markers as a reminder at transition points.

To transition from marl to single strand, simply pick up or drop yarn B and work in pattern as directed. There is no need to cross yarns at back of work, and no holes, gaps or funny spots will appear. It's that easy!

PATTERN BEGINS
Note: Wind small amounts of yarn B onto both yarn bobbins. These will need to be topped up throughout knitting.

BACK
Using yarn A only and long-tail cast-on method, loosely cast on 94 (102, 110, 118, 126, 134) sts.

Ribbing
First and last 6 sts of every row are worked in Seed Stitch with yarns A and B held together (DRS); sts between markers are worked in yarn A only.
Row 1 (RS): Sl1 wyif, [k1, p1] twice, k1, PM, [k2, p2] to last 8 sts, k2, PM, k1, [p1, k1] twice, k1.
Row 2 (WS): Sl1 wyif, [k1, p1] twice, k1, SM, [p2, k2] to 2 sts before marker, p2, SM, k1, [p1, k1] twice, k1.
Row 3 (RS): Sl1 wyif, [k1, p1] twice, k1, SM, [k2, p2] to 2 sts before marker, k2, SM, k1, [p1, k1] twice, k1.
Rep rows 2-3 for 6.5 cm / 2½", ending with a WS row.

SHORT VERSION ONLY
Next Row (RS): Sl1 wyif, [k1, p1] twice, k1, SM, k to marker, SM, k1 [p1, k1] twice, k1.
Next Row (WS): Sl1 wyif, [k1, p1] twice, k1, SM, p to marker, SM, k1, [p1, k1] twice, k1.

LONG VERSION ONLY
Body Side Slit
Next Row (RS): Sl1 wyif, [k1, p1] twice, k1, SM, k to marker, SM, k1, [p1, k1] twice, k1.
Next Row (WS): Sl1 wyif, [k1, p1] twice, k1, SM, p to marker, SM, k1, [p1, k1] twice, k1.
Rep last 2 rows until work measures 30.5 cm / 12" from cast-on edge, ending with a WS row.

BOTH VERSIONS AGAIN
Cast on for Side Notch
Row 1 (RS): PM, with yarns A and B held together and using the

cable method, cast on 12 sts to LH needle. With both yarns held together, [p1, k1] 9 times (slipping marker as you pass it), SM, with yarn A only, k to marker, SM, with both yarns held together, [k1, p1] 3 times. *106 (114, 122, 130, 138, 146) sts*
Row 2 (WS): PM, with yarns A and B held together and cable method, cast on 12 sts to LH needle. With both yarns held together, [p1, k1] 9 times (slipping marker as you pass it), SM, with yarn A only, p to marker, SM, with both yarns held together, [k1, p1] to end (slipping marker as you pass it). *118 (126, 134, 142, 150, 158) sts*
Work first and last 18 sts of each row with yarns A and B held together, continuing in yarn A between centre markers as set. Slip markers as you pass them.
Row 3 (RS): [P1, k1] to second marker, SM, k to marker, SM, [k1, p1] to end.
Row 4 (WS): [P1, k1] to second marker, SM, p to marker, SM, [k1, p1] to end.
Rep rows 3-4 once more, then work row 3 **only** once more.

Sts outside first and last markers will now be worked in yarn A and St st only, with 6 sts between pairs of markers worked in Seed Stitch with yarns A and B held together as set (DRS).
Next row (WS): P to marker, SM, DRS to marker, SM, p to marker, SM, DRS to marker, SM, p to end.
Next row (RS): K to marker, SM, DRS to marker, SM, k to marker, SM, DRS to marker, SM, k to end.

Notch Decrease Row (RS): K to 2 sts before marker, ssk, SM, DRS, SM, k to marker, SM, DRS, SM, k2tog, k to end. *2 sts dec*
Work straight in patt for 5 rows.
Rep last 6 rows a further 8 times. *3 sts rem before first and after last marker*

Armpit Notch
Armpit notch is worked over the last 12 rows of body. Each RS row, DRS sts 'take over' one centre body stitch.
Row 1 (RS): Patt to 2 sts before marker, ssk, SM, DRS, remove marker, p1, PM, patt to 1 st before next marker, PM, p1, remove marker, DRS, SM, k2tog, patt to end. *2 sts dec*
Row 2 (WS): Patt to end, incorporating additional p1 st into DRS.
Row 3 (RS): Patt to marker, SM, DRS to marker, remove marker, p1, PM, patt to 1 st before next marker, PM, p1, remove marker, DRS, SM, patt to end.
Rows 4-6: Rep rows 2-3 once more, then row 2 **only** once more.
Rep rows 1-6 once more. *2 sts dec; 1 st rem before first and after last marker*

Next Row (RS): Removing first and last markers, ssk, patt to last 2 sts, k2tog. *94 (102, 110, 118, 126, 134) sts*
Work 1 WS row straight in patt.
Short Version measures approx. 26.5 cm / 10½"; Long Version measures approx. 57 cm / 22½".

Shape Raglans
Next row (RS): Cast off 6 sts in pattern, DRS to marker, SM, k to marker, SM, DRS to end. *88 (96, 104, 112, 120, 128) sts*
Next row (WS): Cast off 6 sts in pattern, DRS, SM, p to marker, SM, DRS. *82 (90, 98, 106, 114, 122) sts*
Continue in patt as set and work Raglan shaping as foll:
Raglan Dec Row (RS): DRS, SM, k2, k2tog, k to 4 sts before marker, ssk, k2, SM, DRS. *2 sts dec*
Rep Raglan dec row every foll 6th row a further 7 (6, 4, 4, 0, 0) times, then every 4th row 5 (5, 6, 5, 10, 7) times, then every 2nd row 3 (8, 13, 16, 19, 26) times. *50 (50, 50, 54, 54, 54) sts*
Work 1 WS row straight in patt.

Back Collar
Row 1 (RS): DRS, SM, [p2, k2] to 2 sts before marker, p2, SM, DRS.
Row 2 (WS): DRS, SM, [k2, p2] to 2 sts before marker, k2, SM, DRS.
Rep rows 1-2 until collar measures approx. 12.5 cm / 5" or until desired length.
Cast off all sts loosely in pattern.

FRONT
Using yarn A and long-tail method, loosely cast on 82 (90, 98, 106, 114, 122) sts.
Work ribbing as for Back.

SHORT VERSION ONLY
Next Row (RS): Sl1 wyif, [k1, p1] twice, k1, SM, k to marker, SM, k1, [p1, k1] twice, k1.
Next Row (WS): Sl1 wyif, [k1, p1] twice, k1, SM, p to marker, SM, k1, [p1, k1] twice, k1.

LONG VERSION ONLY
Body Side Slit
Next Row (RS): Sl1 wyif, [k1, p1] twice, k1, SM, k to marker, SM, k1 [p1, k1] twice, k1.
Next Row (WS): Sl1 wyif, [k1, p1] twice, k1, SM, p to marker, SM, k1, [p1, k1] twice, k1.
Rep last 2 rows until work measures 30.5 cm / 12" from cast-on edge, ending with a WS row.

BOTH VERSIONS AGAIN
Note: Read through the following section carefully as two sets of instructions are worked **AT THE SAME TIME**.

Front Body
Inc row (RS): DRS, SM, k2, M1L, k to 2 sts before marker, M1R, k2, SM, DRS. *2 sts inc*
Rep Inc row every 12th row a further 5 times. *94 (102, 110, 118, 126, 134) sts*

AT THE SAME TIME
When body measures same as Back to beginning of Armpit Notch:
Row 1 (RS): Patt to marker, SM, DRS, remove marker, p1, PM, patt to 1 st before marker, PM, p1, remove marker, DRS, SM, patt to end.
Row 2 (WS): Patt to end, incorporating additional p1 st into DRS.
Rep rows 1-2 a further 4 times.

Shape Raglans
Cast off for underarms and work Raglan dec row as for Back until 11 (12, 17, 19, 24, 28) Raglan dec rows have been worked, ending after a WS row. *60 (66, 64, 68, 66, 66) sts*

Neck Shaping
Left and Right Fronts are now worked separately and short rows are worked on each side to shape front neck.
Continue to work Raglan dec rows as set to match Back, and shape neck as follows:

Left Front
Row 1 (RS): Patt 27 (27, 29, 29, 31, 31) sts, w&t.
Row 2 (WS): Patt to end.
Row 3 (RS): Patt to 2 sts before w&t, w&t.
Rep rows 2-3 a further 5 times. Work Row 2 **only** once more.
End with a WS Row, but do not work DRS. Break yarn A, leave yarn B attached.

Right Front
Row 1 (RS): With RS facing, rejoin yarn A after first wrap and turn on Left Front and patt to end.
Row 2 (WS): Patt 27 (27, 29, 29, 31, 31) sts, w&t.
Row 3 (RS): Patt to end.
Row 4 (WS): Patt to 2 sts before w&t, w&t.
Rep rows 3-4 a further 5 times. Work row 3 **only** once more.

Next row (WS): Patt to end, picking up wraps from the RS and purling them tog with their wrapped st.

Front Collar
Work as for Back.

SLEEVES
Cuff
Using yarn A and long-tail method, loosely cast on 42 (42, 46, 46, 50, 50) sts.
Row 1 (RS): [P1, k1] 3 times, PM, [p2, k2] to last 8 sts, p2, PM, [k1, p1] 3 times.
Row 2 (WS): DRS, SM, [k2, p2] to 2 sts before marker, k2, SM, DRS.
Row 3 (RS): DRS, SM, [p2, k2] to 2 sts before marker, p2, SM, DRS.
Rep rows 2-3 until cuff measures 6.5 cm / 2½" from cast-on edge, ending with a WS row.

First and last 6 sts of each row are worked as DRS. Centre sts between markers are worked in St st and yarn A.
Inc Row (RS): DRS, SM, k2, M1L, k to 2 sts before marker, M1R, k2, SM, DRS. *2 sts inc*
Continue in patt as set, working Inc Row every 8 (8, 8, 6, 6, 6)th row a further 9 (3, 0, 10, 9, 6) times, then every 6 (6, 6, 4, 4, 4)th row 2 (10, 14, 6, 8, 13) times. *66 (70, 76, 80, 86, 90) sts*

Work straight until sleeve measures 40 cm / 15½" from cast-on edge, ending with a WS row.

Shape Raglans
Next row (RS): Cast off 6 sts in pattern, remove marker and break yarn B, patt to marker, SM, DRS. *60 (64, 70, 74, 80, 84) sts*
Next row (WS): Cast off 6 sts in pattern, remove marker and break yarn B, patt to end. *54 (58, 64, 68, 74, 78) sts*
Remainder of sleeve is worked in yarn A and St st.
Sleeve Dec Row (RS): K2, k2tog, k to last 4 sts, ssk, k2. *2 sts dec*
Continue in St st, working Dec row every foll 4th row a further 9 (9, 7, 6, 5, 4) times, then every 2nd row 16 (18, 23, 26, 30, 33) times. *2 sts*
Cast off rem 2 sts.

FINISHING
Block pieces to measurements before seaming.
Sew seams using mattress stitch and weave in ends.
A. Bust circumference: 93.5 (101.5, 109, 117.5, 125.5, 133.5) cm /

36¾ (40, 43, 46¼, 49½, 52½)"
B. Total Length Short: 50 (51.5, 52, 53, 54, 54.5) cm / 19¾ (20¼, 20½, 20¾, 21¼, 21½)"
C: Total Length Long: 80.5 (81.5, 82.5, 83, 84.5, 85) cm / 31¾ (32¼, 32½, 32¾, 33¼, 33½)"
D: Back neck width: 25.5 (25.5, 25.5, 27.5, 27.5, 27.5) cm / 10 (10, 10, 10¾, 10¾, 10¾)"
E: Raglan depth: 23.5 (24.5, 25.5, 26.5, 28, 28.5) cm / 9¼ (9¾, 10, 10½, 11, 11¼)"
F: Upper sleeve: 33.5 (35.5, 38.5, 40.5, 44, 48.5) cm / 13¼ (14, 15¼, 16, 17¼, 18)"
G: Lower sleeve: 21.5 (21.5, 23.5, 23.5, 25.5, 25.5) cm / 8½ (8½, 9¼, 9¼, 10, 10)"
H: Sleeve length: 40 cm / 15½"

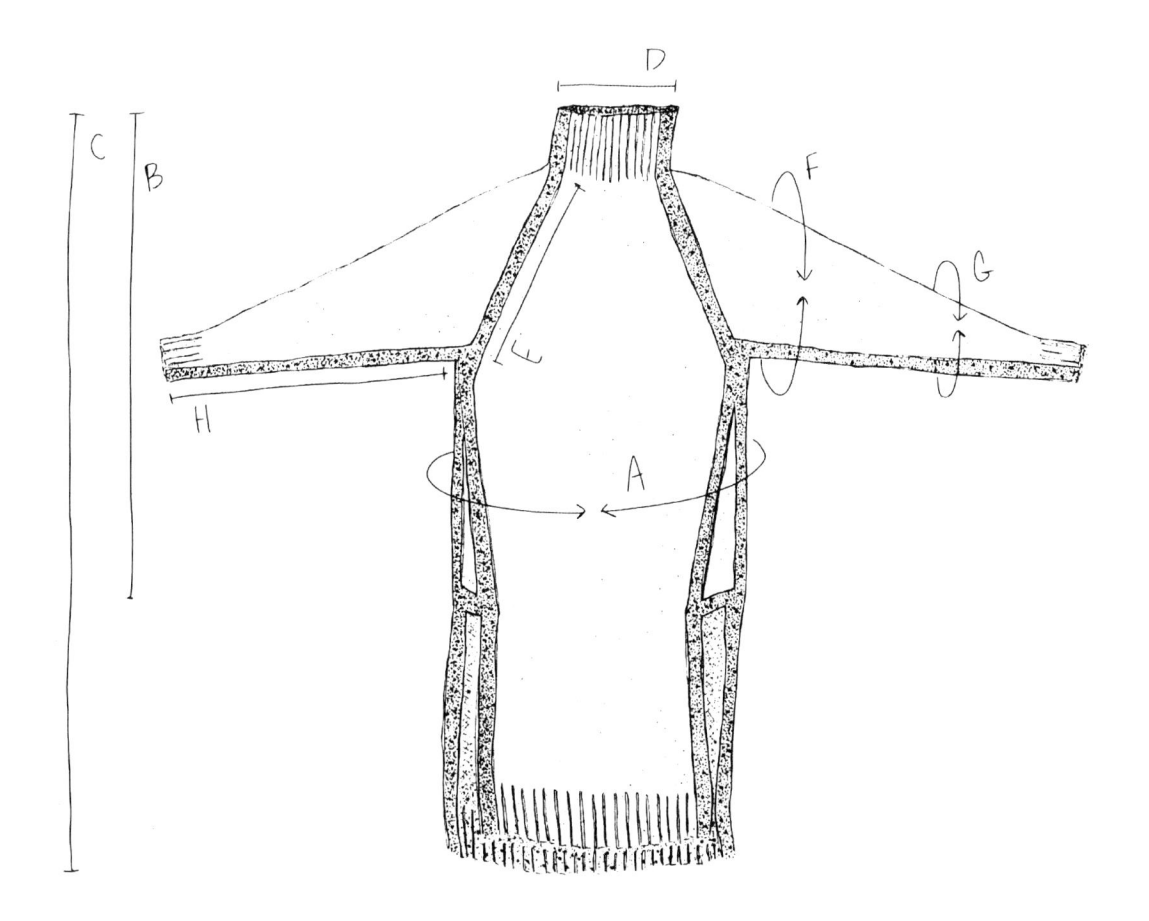

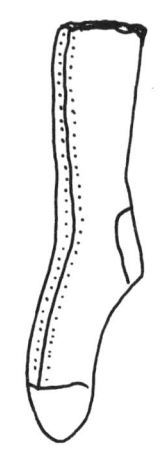

favourite sock variations

As their name suggests, these are truly my most favourite socks. I published the original pattern about three years ago and haven't stopped knitting it since. With each new pair, I experiment with colour placement, stripe and texture. One colour combination leads straight into the next, and I love the blank canvas these basic ribbed socks provide. It allows for endless experimentation and play.

Here I have updated the pattern, adding smaller and larger sizes as well as some variations to the original 3 x 1 ribbed pattern. Like my stripes, I could create an indefinite number of Favourite Sock variations, and I hope that this pattern inspires you to create some of your own. Just be warned that these socks can be dangerously addictive!

113

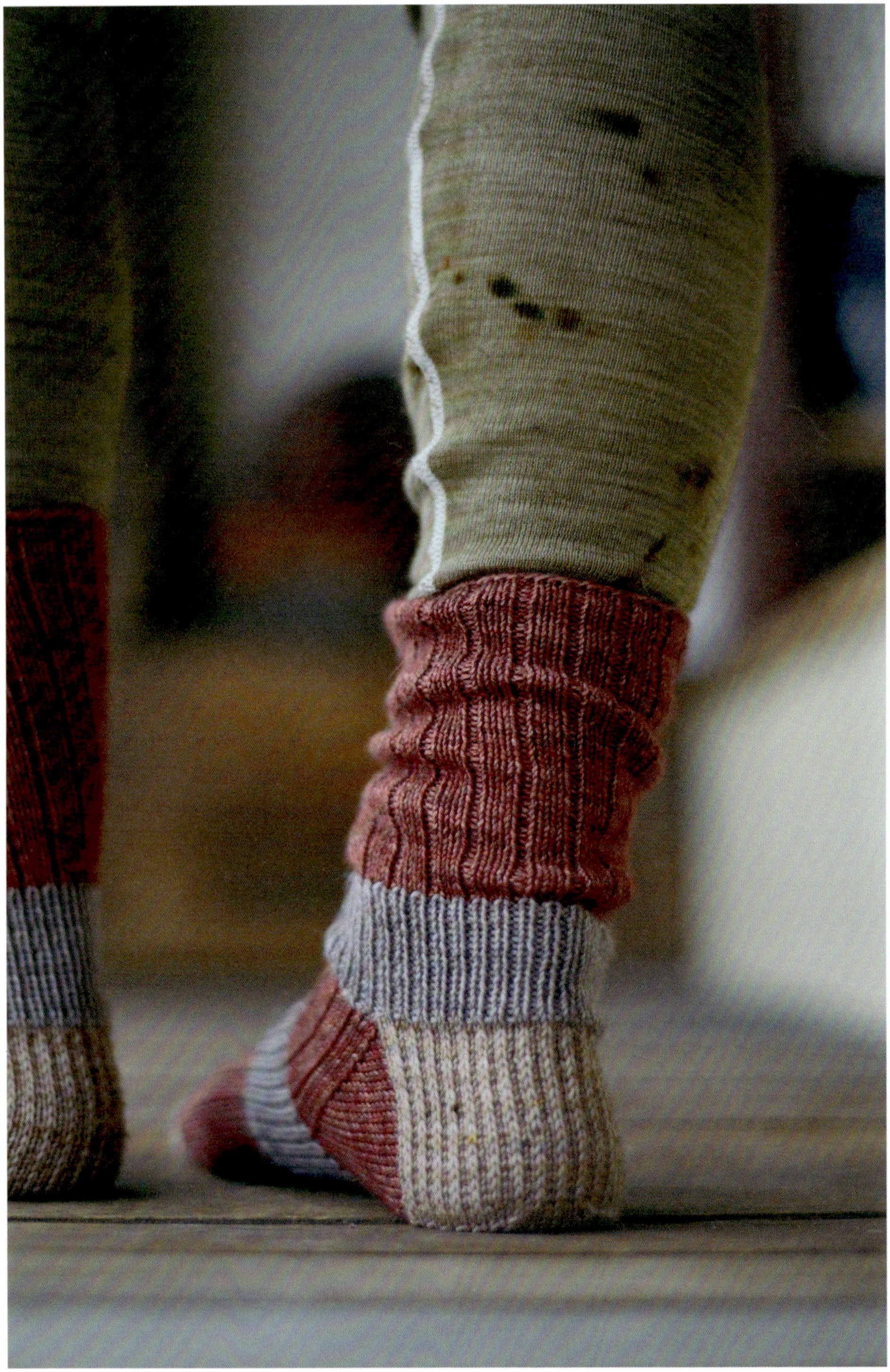

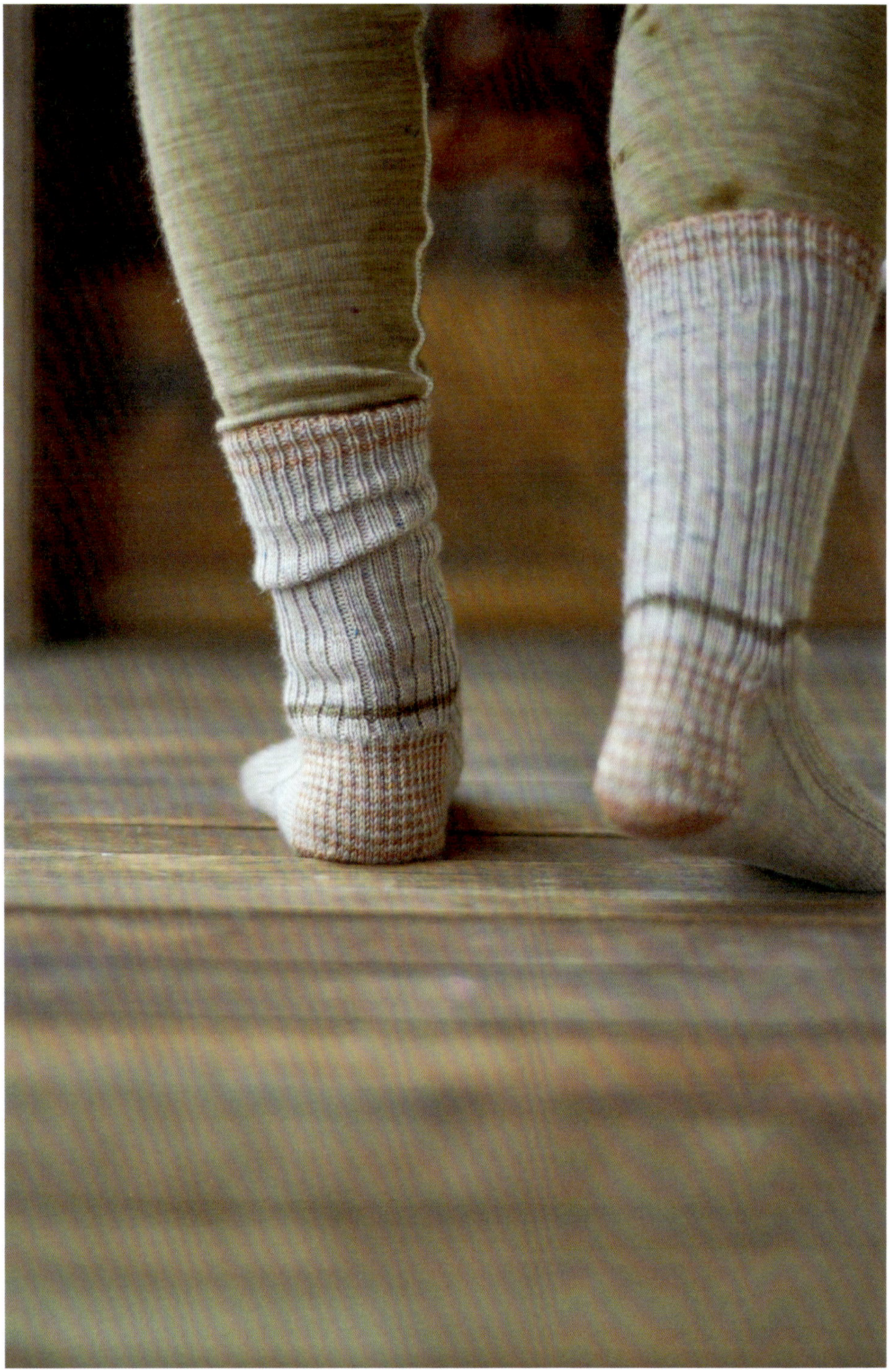

Favourite Sock Variation

Sizes: 1 (2, 3, 4, 5)
Finished circumference, relaxed: 14 (14.5, 16, 16.5, 17) cm / 5½ (5¾, 6¼, 6½, 6¾)"
All sample socks knit in size 1, measurements taken at cuff.
Yarn: Viola Sock (4 ply / fingering weight; 75% Superwash Merino, 25% Nylon; 421 m / 460 yds per 100 g skein)
and / or
Viola Sock Minis (4 ply / fingering weight; 75% Superwash Merino, 25% Nylon; 85 m / 93 yds per 20 g skein)
Note: For a pair, you will need a total of approximately 100 (105, 110, 115, 120) g or about 420 (440, 460, 480, 500) m / 460 (480, 505, 525, 550) yds
Shades:
Version A
C1: Giant Peach; 64 (66, 68, 73, 75) m / 70 (72, 75, 80, 83) yds
C2: Silver Birch; 315 (330, 347, 362, 379) m / 345 (360, 380, 395, 415) yds
C3: Eclipse; 42 (44, 46, 48, 51) m / 46 (48, 50, 53, 56) yds
Version B
C1: Eclipse; 42 (44, 46, 48, 51) m / 46 (48, 50, 53, 56) yds
C2: Spruce; 21 (22, 23, 24, 25) m / 23 (24, 25, 26, 27) yds
C3: Deep Earth; 315 (330, 347, 362, 379) m / 345 (360, 380, 395, 415) yds
Version C
C1: Eclipse; 126 (132, 139, 145, 151) m / 138 (145, 152, 159, 165) yds
C2: Fireside; 84 (88, 92, 97, 100) m / 92 (96, 101, 106, 110) yds
C3: Giant Peach; 126 (132, 139, 145, 151) m / 138 (145, 152, 159, 165) yds
Version D
C1: Fireside; 252 (265, 278, 290, 303) m / 276 (290, 304, 317, 332) yds
C2: Moonrock; 64 (66, 68, 73, 75) m / 70 (72, 75, 80, 83) yds
C3: Giant Peach; 64 (66, 68, 73, 75) m / 70 (72, 75, 80, 83) yds
Gauge: 52 sts & 52 rnds = 10 cm / 4" over 3x1 rib on 2.25 mm needles, after blocking
50 sts & 46 rnds = 10 cm / 4" over 1x1 rib on 2.25 mm needles, after blocking
Gauge measurements taken while fabric is completely relaxed.
Needles: 2.25 mm / US 1 knitting needles suitable for working small circumferences in the round.
Always use a needle size that will result in the correct gauge after blocking.
Notions: Stitch markers, cable needle for Version B, tapestry needle
Notes: This is an updated, improved, and expanded version of my original, Emily's Favourite Socks Pattern. My Favourite Socks are very simple; I cannot take any credit for the original idea.
They're knit from the cuff down in 3x1 ribbing, with a classic heel flap and short row heel. I love to play around with adding contrasting heels, toes and stripes to each pair and have added 4 variations to the original 3x1 rib to provide a few different options for stitch pattern and placement. This updated version of the pattern also includes two additional sizes. When choosing a size, keep in mind that the sock must be able to stretch over your heel and not just your ankle or foot and that tight socks make for cold feet! I prefer that my socks fit with about ¼" positive ease, but these socks will fit comfortably ranging from ½" negative ease to ½" positive ease. I like to err on the larger side, so that I don't have to wrestle into my socks every day.
Please note that each version fit with slightly different ease. 1x1 ribbing makes for the most elastic leg, while the cable pattern in Version B creates the tightest fit, and stretches the least.
Notes in pattern indicate when to change colours for each version, but these are only guidelines. Please experiment with amount of colours and placement of stripes - the options are endless!

Stitch Glossary for Basic Socks:
1x1 Rib (optional cuff)
Round 1: [K1, p1] to end.
Rep round 1 for pattern.

3x1 Rib (Body)
Round 1: [K3, p1] to end.
Rep round 1 for pattern.

PATTERN BEGINS (make 2)
LEG
Using long-tail method, cast on 72 (76, 80, 84, 88) sts. Join for working in the round, being careful not to twist sts. PM to indicate beg of round.

Basic Sock
Work 1x1 Rib for 3.5 cm / 1½".
Work 3x1 Rib until leg measures 17 cm / 6¾" from cast-on edge, or desired length.

Variations
Work in chosen pattern & colour(s) until leg measures 17 cm / 6¾" from cast-on edge, or to desired length.

HEEL
Sts will now be rearranged to prepare for working Heel Flap and turn. First 35 (39, 39, 43, 43) sts will be referred to as Heel Sts, and will be worked while remaining 37 (37, 41, 41, 45) Instep sts are held to be worked when rejoining foot. Rearrange sts on needles so that Instep sts are separate from Heel sts. It will be important to keep Instep and Heel sts separate for remainder of pattern. There should be a purl st at beg and end of Instep sts.

Heel Flap
Row 1 (RS): [Sl 1 pwise wyib, k1] 17 (19, 19, 21, 21) times to last st, cast on 1 st using backwards loop method, k1, turn. *36 (40, 40, 44, 44) sts for Heel Flap; 73 (77, 81, 85, 89) sts total*
Row 2 (WS): Sl1 pwise wyif, p to end of Heel Flap.
Row 3 (RS): [Sl1 wyib, k1] to end.
Rep rows 2-3 a further 16 (18, 18, 20, 20) times, then work row 2 once more. *36 (40, 40, 44, 44) total rows*

Heel Turn
Set-up row 1 (RS): K23 (25, 25, 29, 29), ssk, k1, turn.
Set-up row 2 (WS): Sl1 pwise, p11 (11, 11, 15, 15) sts, p2tog, p1, turn.
Row 1 (RS): Sl1 wyib, k to 1 st before gap, ssk, k1, turn.
Row 2 (WS): Sl1 wyif, p to 1 st before gap, p2tog, p1, turn.
Rep rows 1-2 a further 4 (5, 5, 5, 5) times. *24 (26, 26, 30, 30) sts*

GUSSET
Pick Up Gusset (RS): K12 (13, 13, 15, 15) heel sts, PM for new beg of round. Pick up and knit 19 (21, 21, 23, 23) sts in the slipped sts on the right side of the heel flap, pick up and knit 1 st to close the gap between heel flap and instep, patt across 37 (37, 41, 41, 45) instep sts, pick up and knit 1 st to close the gap between heel flap and instep, pick up and knit 19 (21, 21, 23, 23) sts along left side of heel flap, k to end of round. *101 (107, 111, 119, 123) sts*

Centre bottom of foot is now beg of Round. Redistribute sts if needed, ensuring that Instep and Heel/Bottom of Foot sts remain separate.

Decrease for Gusset
Set-up round: K12 (13, 13, 15, 15), ktbl across next 20 (22, 22, 24, 24) sts, PM, patt across Instep sts, PM, ktbl across next 20 (22, 22, 24, 24) sts, k to end.
Round 1 (Dec): K to 4 sts before marker, k2tog, k2, SM, patt across Instep sts, SM, k2, ssk, k to end. *2 sts dec*
Round 2: K to marker, SM, patt across Instep sts, SM, k to end.
Rep rounds 1-2 a further 13 (14, 14, 16, 16) times. *73 (77, 81, 85, 89) sts*
Final Decrease Round: K to 4 sts before marker, k2tog, k2, SM, patt across Instep sts, SM, k to end. *72 (76, 80, 84, 88) sts*

FOOT
Continue straight in pattern until foot measures 14 (14.5, 15, 15.5) cm / 5½ (5¾, 6, 6¼, 6½)" or about 4.5 (4.5, 5, 5, 5) cm / 1¾ (1¾, 2, 2, 2)" short of desired length.

TOE
Round 1 (Dec): *K to 4 sts before marker, k2tog k2, SM, k2, ssk; rep from * once more, k to end. *4 sts dec*
Round 2: Knit.
Rep rounds 1-2 a further 10 (11, 11, 12, 13) times, then work round 1 once more. *24 (24, 28, 28, 28) sts*
Break yarn leaving a 25 cm / 10" tail.

FINISHING
Graft Toe sts and weave in all ends.

VARIATIONS
Stitch Glossary
1/2 RC: Slip 2 sts to cable needle and hold in back, k1, k2 from cable needle.
1/2 LC: Slip 1 st to cable needle and hold in front, k2, k1 from cable needle.

Version A: 1x1 Ribbed Column, sizes 1 (3, 5) only
Round 1: *[K1, p1] 3 (3, 4) times, [k3, p1] 6 (7, 7) times, [k1, p1] 3 (3, 4) times; rep from * once more.
Rep round 1 for pattern.

Version B: Cable Column in 1x1 Rib (All Sizes)
Rounds 1-3: *[K1, p1] 6 (6, 7, 7, 8) times, k 0 (1, 0, 1, 0), [k3, p1] 3 times, k (0, 1, 0, 1, 0), [k1, p1] 6 (6, 7, 7, 8) times; rep from * once more.
Cable Set-up Round: *[K1, p1] 6 (6, 7, 7, 8) times, k 0 (1, 0, 1, 0), 1/2 RC, p1, k3, p1, 1/2 LC, p1, k 0 (1, 0, 1, 0), [k1, p1] 6 (6, 7, 7, 8) times; rep from * once more.
Rounds 5-7: Rep rounds 1-3.
Round 8: *[K1, p1] 6 (6, 7, 7, 8) times, k 0 (1, 0, 1, 0), 1/2 RC, p1, [k1, p1] 2 times, 1/2 LC, p1, k 0 (1, 0, 1, 0), [k1, p1] 6 (6, 7, 7, 8) times; rep from * once more.
Rep rounds 5-8 for pattern.

Version B: Cable Column in 3x1 Rib (Sizes 1 (5) only)
Rounds 1-3: [K3, p1] to end.
Round 4 (Cable Set-up): *[K3, p1] 3 (4) times, 1/2 RC, p1, k3, p1, 1/2 LC, p1, [k3, p1] 3 (4) times; rep from * once more.
Rounds 5-7: Rep rounds 1-3.
Round 8: *[K3, p1] 3 (4) times, 1/2 RC, p1, [k1, p1] 2 times, 1/2 LC, p1, [k3, p1] 3 (4) times; rep from * once more.
Rep rounds 5-8 for pattern

Version B: Cable Column in 3x1 Rib (Size 3 only)
Rounds 1-3: *[K3, p1] 3 times, k1, p1, [k3, p1] 3 times, k1, p1, [k3, p1] 3 times; rep from * once more.
Cable set-up round: *[K3, p1] 3 times, k1, p1, 1/2 RC, p1, k3, p1, 1/2 LC, p1, k1, p1, [k3, p1] 3 times; rep from * once more.
Rounds 5-7: Rep rounds 1-3.

Favourite Sock Variation

Round 8: *[K3, p1] 3 times, k1, p1, 1/2 RC, p1, [k1, p1] 2 times, 1/2 LC, p1, k1, p1, [k3, p1] 3 times; rep from * once more.
Rep rounds 5-8 for pattern.

PATTERN AND COLOUR NOTES
Version A - Ribbed Column, sizes 1 (3, 5) only:
Cuff: Cast on with C1.
Work 1x1 Rib in C1 for 2 rounds.
Work 1x1 Ribg in C2 for 2 rounds.
Repeat last 2 rounds twice more. Break C1.
Leg: With C2 only, work in 1x1 Ribbed Column until Leg measures approx. 15 cm / 6" from cast-on edge. Join C3 and work 3 rounds. Break C3. Continue in C2 until Leg measures approx. 17 cm / 6¾" from cast on edge.
Heel Flap and Turn: Work Heel Flap striping C1 and C2 every 2 rows. Work Heel Turn in C1.
Gusset and Foot: Break C1 and work Gusset and Foot in C2 to 2 cm / ¾" before start of Toe. Work Foot in C3 for 3 rounds. Break C3 and work in C2 to end of Foot.
Toe: Work Toe striping C1 and C2 every 2 rounds. Graft toe in C1.

Version B - Cable Columns
Cuff: Cast on with C1 and work Cable Column in 1x1 Ribbing for 3.5 cm / 1½".
Change to C2 and work 1 cm / ¼" in pattern.
Leg, Heel, Gusset, and Foot: Use C3.
All Sizes: Continue working Cable Column in 1x1 Rib throughout.
OPTIONAL: Sizes 1, 3, 5 ONLY: Work Cable Column in 3x1 Rib for your size throughout.

All Sizes, Toe: Work in C3.

Version C - Extra Long Ribbing
Cuff: Cast on with C1 and work 1x1 Rib until Leg measures 15 cm / 6" from cast-on edge. Change to Body Rib and continue in C1 until Leg measures 17 cm / 6¾" from cast-on edge.
Heel Flap and Turn: Work Heel Flap and turn in C2 through to gusset decreases.
Gusset, Foot, and Toe: Continue to work in C2 for first 2.5 cm / 1" of Gusset. Change to C3, and work to end of toe.

Version D - Snug Arch
Cuff: Cast on with C1 and work Body Rib for 13 cm / 5¼" from cast-on edge.
Change to C2 and work 1x1 Rib for 4 cm / 1½".
Heel Flap and Turn: Work Heel Flap and Turn in C3. Rejoin C1 after completion of Heel Turn.

Gusset and Foot: Work in C1 for all of Gusset Decreases. After decreases are complete, break C1 and work 1x1 Rib in C2 for 4 cm / 1½". Continue in Body Rib to end of Foot.
Toe: Work Toe in C3.

A. Finished circumference (relaxed): 14 (14.5, 16, 16.5, 17) cm / 5½ (5¾, 6¼, 6½, 6¾)"
B. Leg length: 17 cm / 6¾"

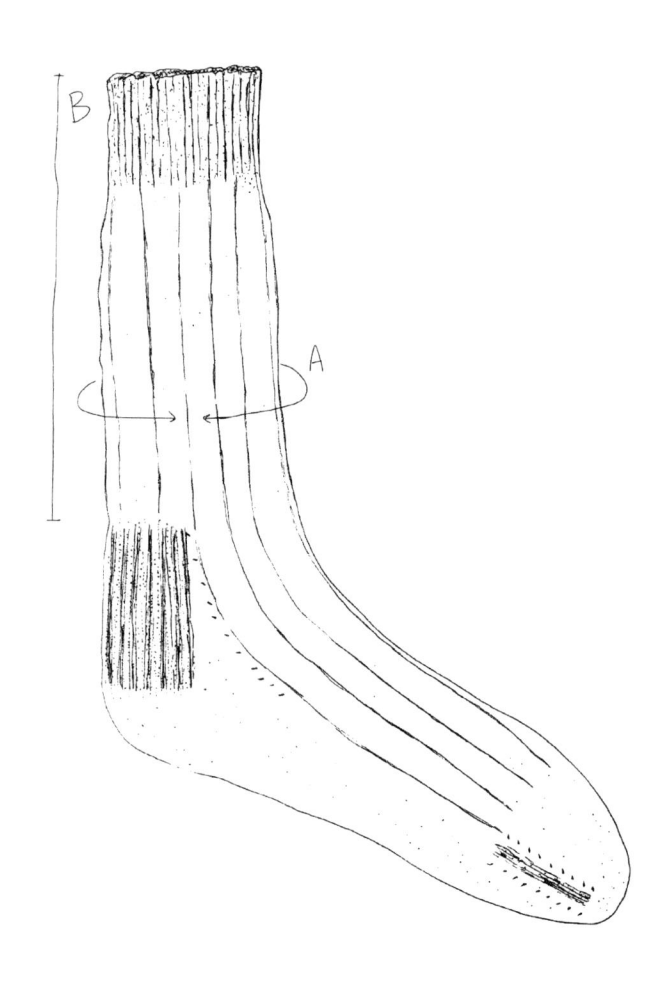

119

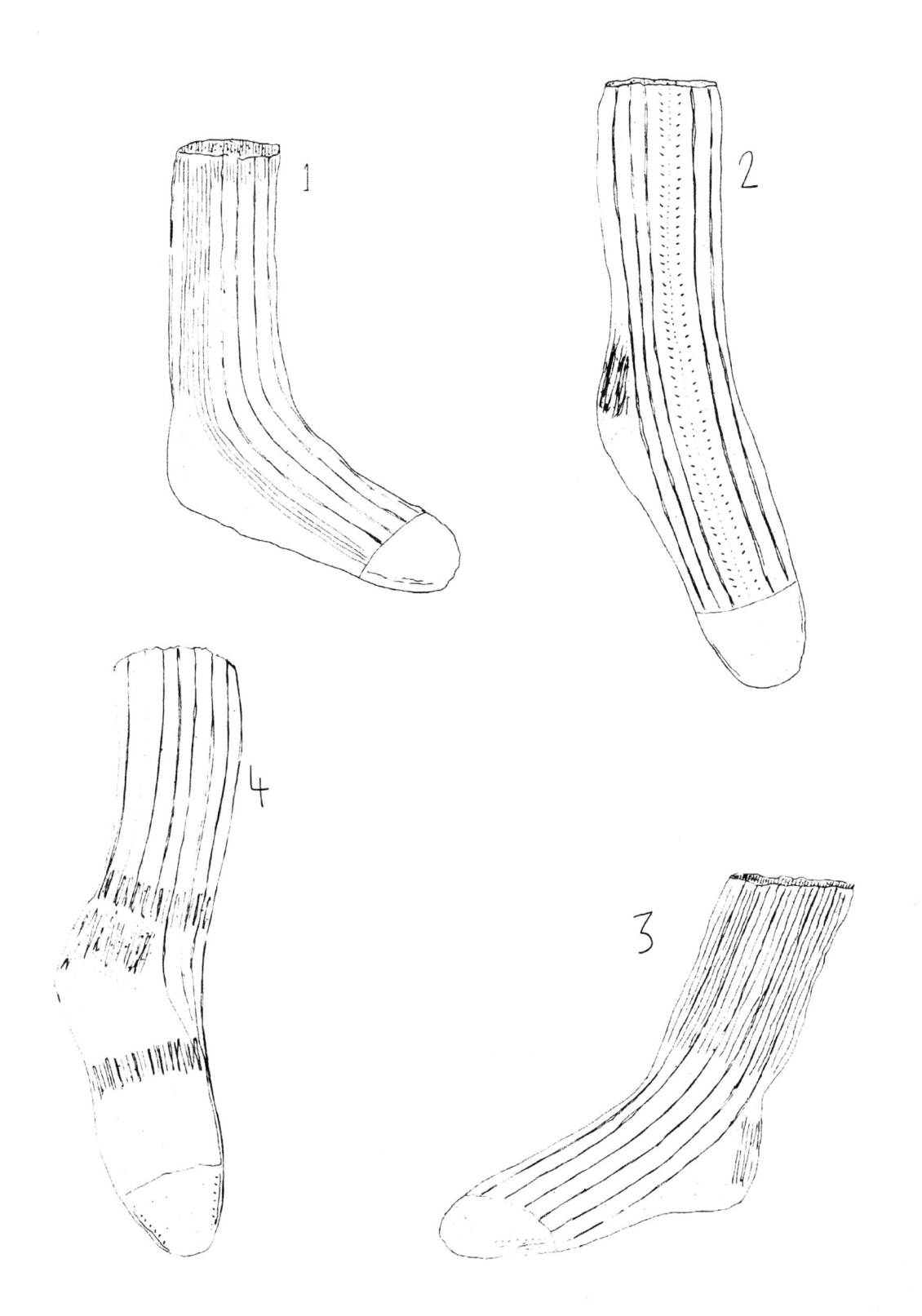

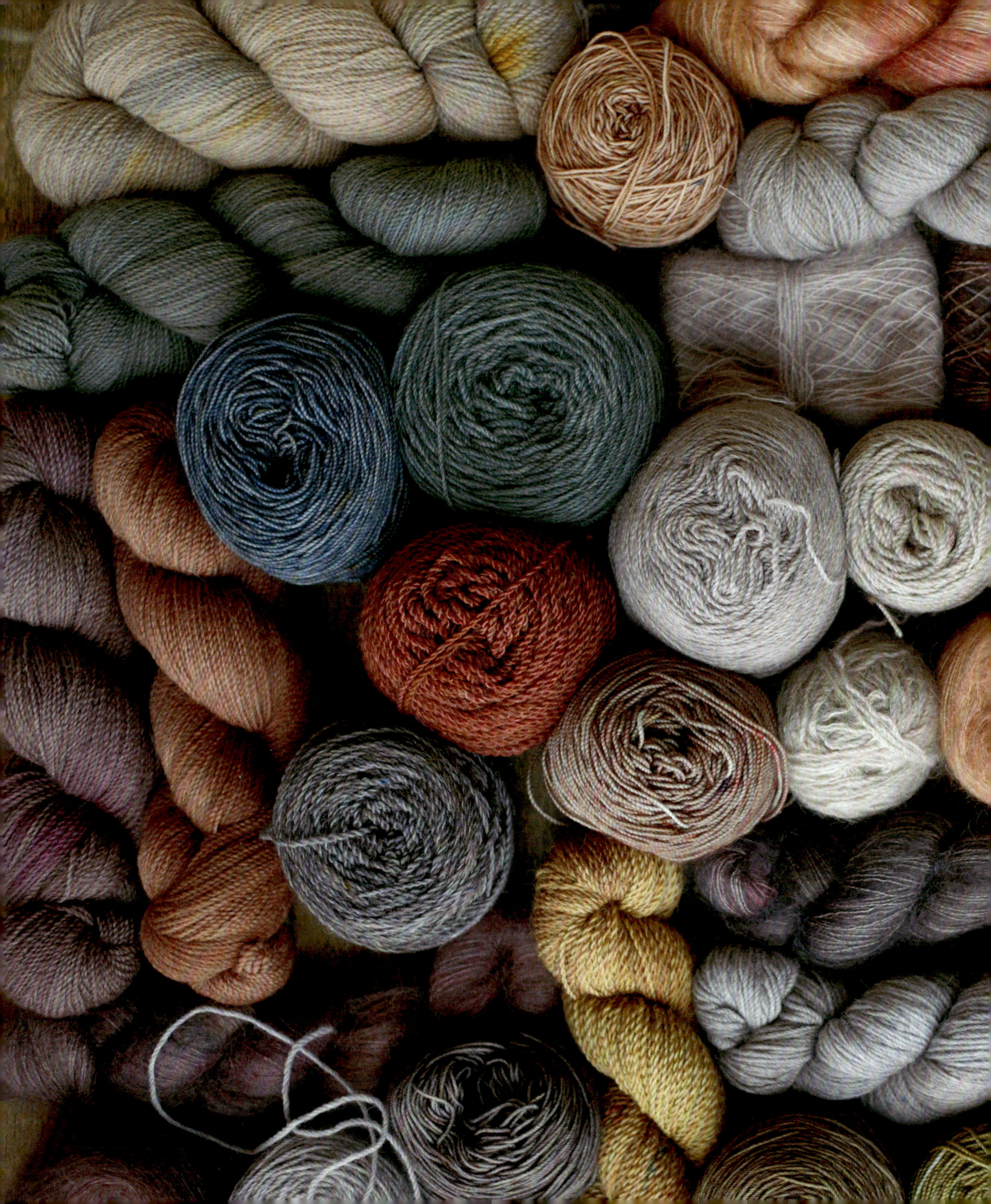

creating the colourways

Viola colourways are not inspired by just one object, photograph or place, but are pieced together from memories and impressions of seasons, weather, landscape, and light.

At times, they can be as changeable as the mist and clouds that inspire them. I constantly study the colours and textures of the world around me, absorbing ideas and colours all the time. I look to the natural world for colour inspiration, taking into account the proportions of colour in a scene, the source and direction of light, clouds, precipitation, time of year and so on. I have created four new colourways for this book and each of them are inspired by different moments and memories of winter in Mooresburg. They are a combination of more than one colour memory, a sort of highlight reel of the colours of winter that stand out to me.

Fireside
There is very little red in the winter landscape, and yet I think of it as an essential winter colour.

Perhaps it's because the tiny hints of red that linger in winter stand out vividly against their snowy surroundings. The flash of a cardinal or bittersweet berry among brown trees is a rare and thrilling sight, and this orange-red colour also happens to be my favourite shade. At the other end of the red spectrum is dogwood, which casts a cool, purple tinge on its surroundings. Dogwood is often found among the warm brown and rust of other shrubs, creating tangles of warm and cool. The wonderful thing about red is that a little goes a long way; even the tiniest fleck draws the eye in. Fireside takes into account all of these reds, layered with brown, rust and shadowy purple, just like my winter landscape.

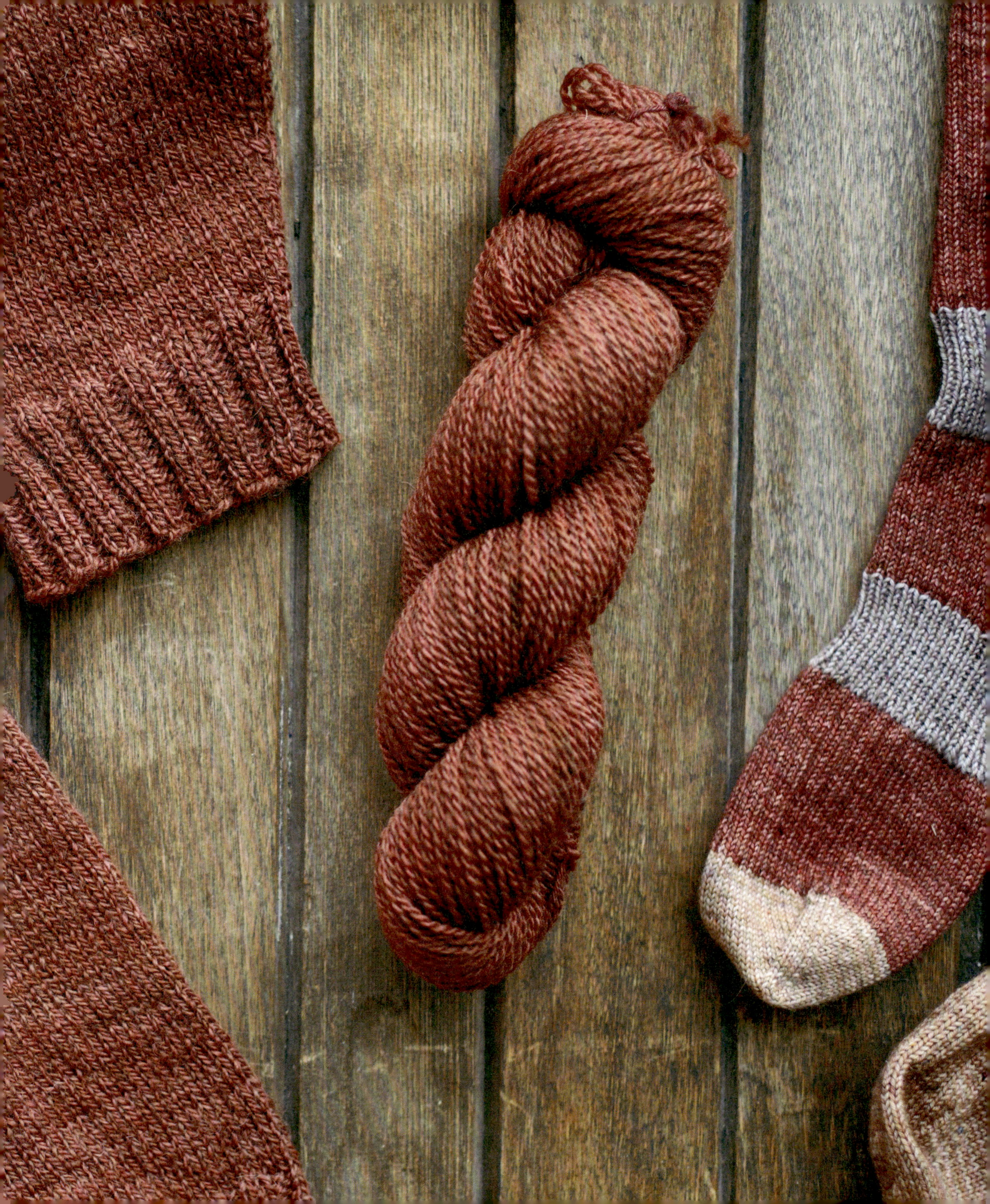

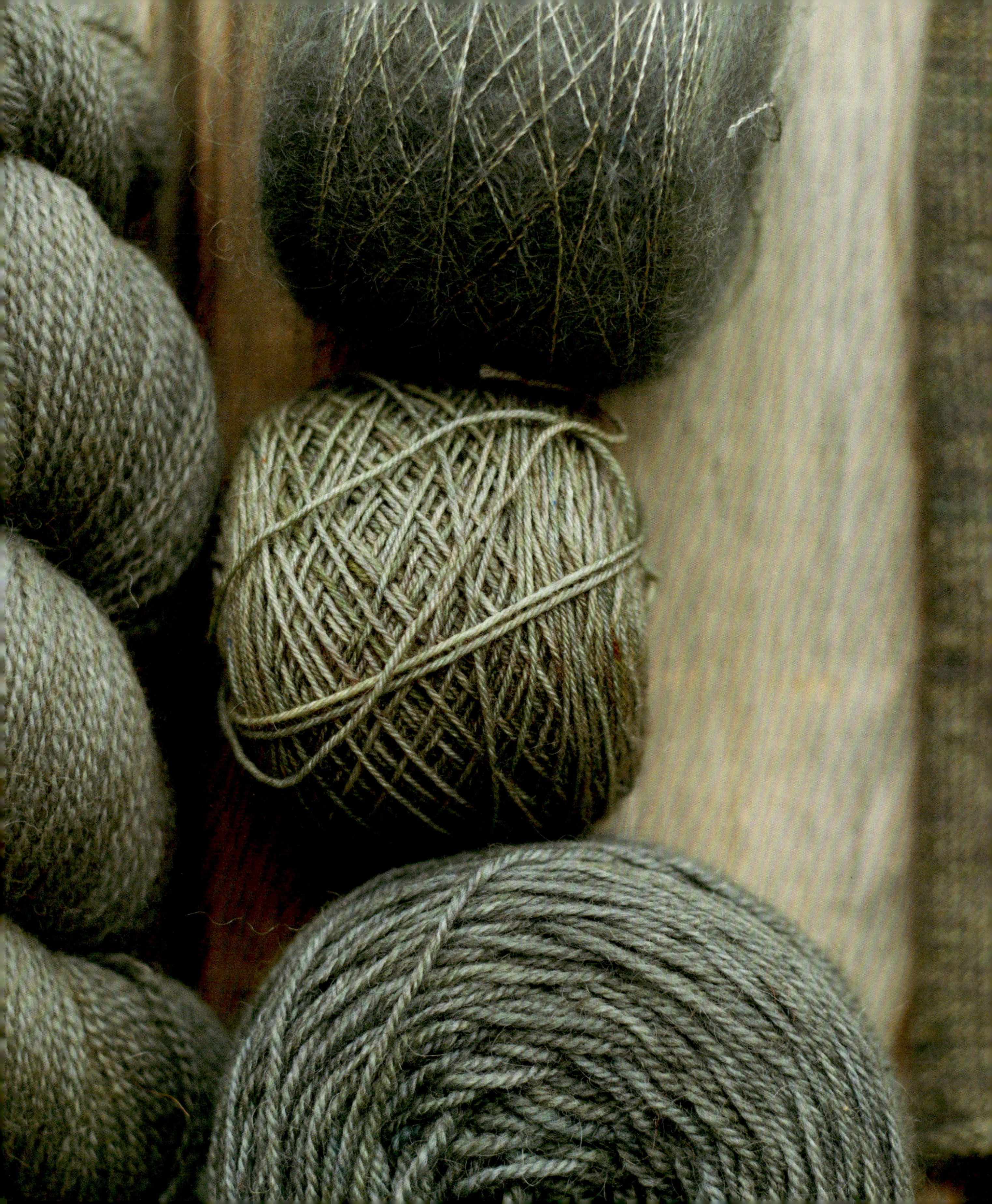

Evergreen

A friend once told me that our human eyes can distinguish more shades of green than any other colour.

While I haven't done a shred of research to support this claim, I certainly have experienced it. Dyeing green has always been tricky for me because the smallest addition of yellow or blue can easily take the colour too far. This makes perfect sense if my eyes can see a greater variety of greens than any other colour.

Green in winter has always interested me. While it dominates the landscape of spring and summer, in winter green lingers only in conifers. Yet the variety of greens that can be found in their needles is huge. There is a beautiful spruce tree outside my kitchen window and as its branches fill with snow, the green of its needles appears to darken in contrast. The colour that pokes out from under the snow looks dark and cold, but up close those same needles contain warm yellows and browns. Evergreen is simply about the colour that is hidden under that snow: a changeable and fleeting green. Once the snow melts, the colour will change again.

Frozen Earth

Brown is an abundant colour in my winter landscape. I know that it is not always the most popular colour, and I must admit that I don't like flat browns much.

However, the browns of winter are rich, complex and beautiful. I first came to admire this colour in trees. On damp days, the rainbow of brown and grey tree trunks becomes rich and deep. I have interrupted many winter runs to inspect tree bark, occasionally lingering too long and catching quite a chill! Another magical brown is in the chunks of overturned earth in a field, perhaps dusted with snow or glistening with frost. Its dark, cold colour is often made up of surprisingly bright purples, blues, greens and gold.

On a misty morning, it is iridescent, glowing and totally amazing. Brown may have a bad rap, but Frozen Earth is made

127

128

Silver Birch

Silver Birch is about bright, light layers of colour, and I think it's the most magical of winter colours.

Take a look at snow, and you will see that it is anything but white: cold blue shadows, golden haze and dusty pink reflections bounce off its surface. Snow is a sparkling mirror of any other colour that is held up to it. Falling snow even softens and obscures the colours of familiar surroundings. A similarly complex variety of pastel colours can be found in birch bark. Starting with an almost invisible pinkish undertone, it is covered by a creamy warm grey that reflects a luminous silvery light. These are colours that are so subtle you might miss them during the more colourful seasons of the year. Winter provides a rare opportunity to see them at their most vivid.

Creating very light colourways using dyes is a tricky job. Unlike mixing paints, creating a light colour with dyes requires using tiny amounts of dye very carefully because there is no way to add white once a colour has gone too dark. This creates a problem for me because white paint has substance; even though it doesn't add colour, it adds depth. The lack of a dye equivalent to white paint often leaves me feeling that light colours are missing layers of white over layers of colour. With this in mind, I set about creating Silver Birch using the most careful amounts of dye. I am really happy with the result and was in awe of the colours that emerged when I knit up a pair of Favourite Socks. I hope you enjoy it too.

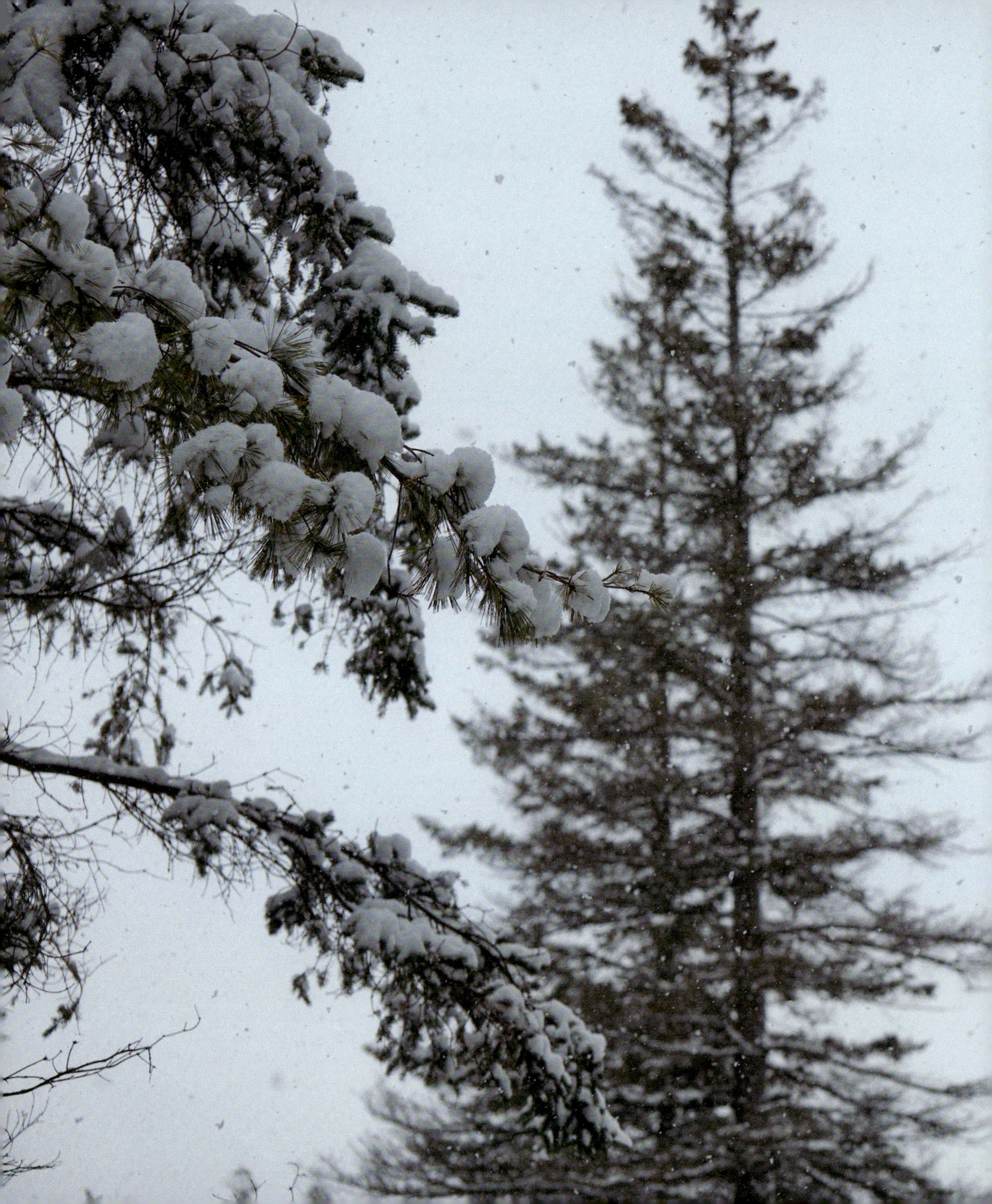

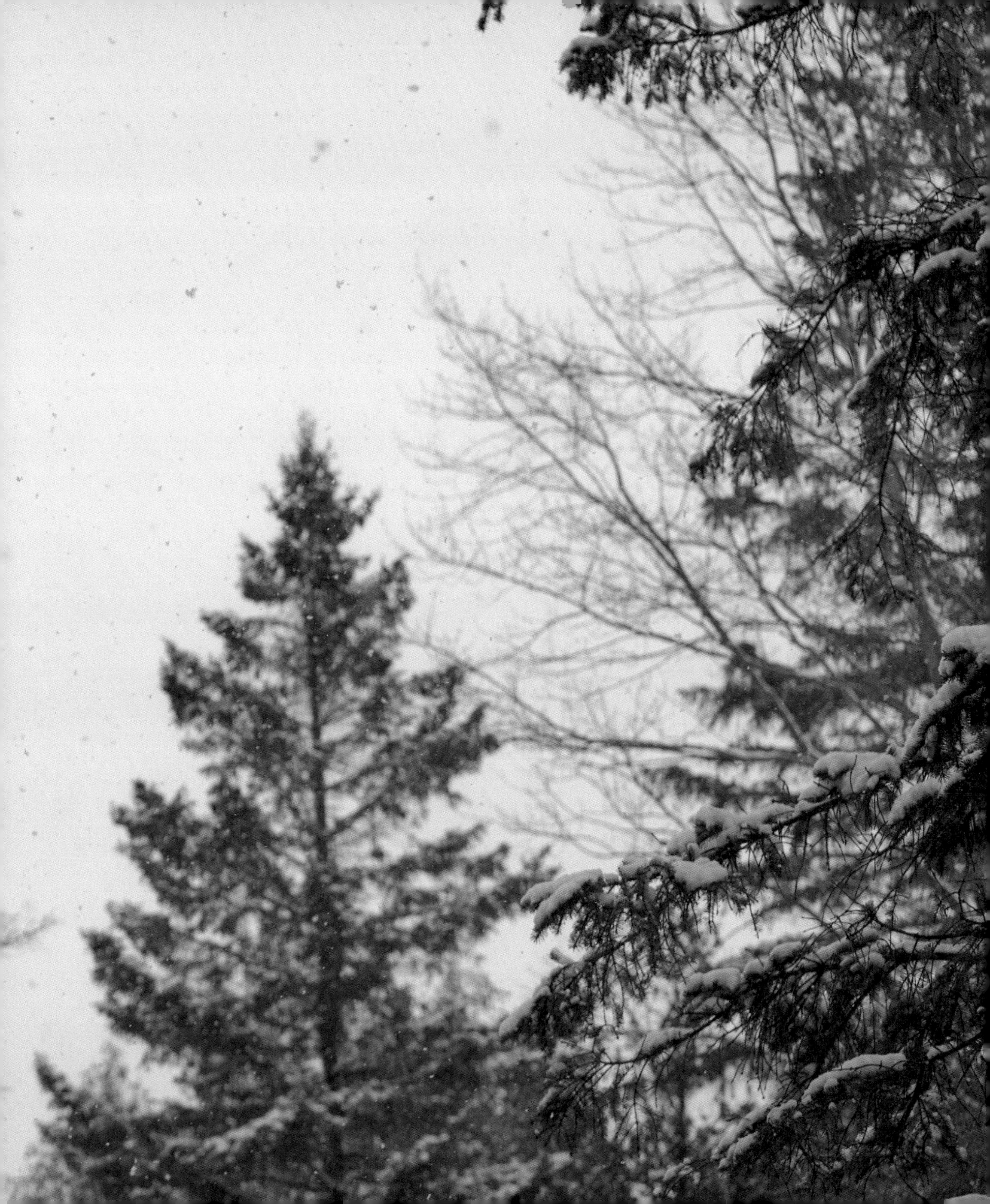

acknowledgements

THANK YOU TO...

Tech Editors Laura Chau and Jemima Bicknell.

Models Kiyomi and Sachiko Burgin who are sisters, makers of beautiful things in their own right, and talented models to boot! In addition to braving the cold during the photoshoot, they both generously contributed their creative energies to this book. Kiyomi knit the Eastwind sample and Sachiko made the delicate silver twig pin shown with Full Moon.

Brittany Piper for keeping Viola going while I was fussing over this book.

Jill Foden for listening to all of my crises and contributing hand lettering.

Don Foden for providing expert camera advice.

Jeremy Freed for reading over my words.

The Mooresburg Community for everyone's ongoing interest in and support of Viola and me.

Violet & Lucy for being themselves.

And of course, THANK YOU to Lydia Gluck, Meghan Fernandes and Amy Collins for this opportunity and for patiently answering thousands of my goofy questions.

abbreviations

beg	Beginning
brk	Knit slipped stitch and yarn over from previous row/round together.
brp	Purl slipped stitch and yarn over from previous row/round together.
cast off	Bind off
CC	Contrast colour
dec	Decrease
DPN(s)	Double-pointed needle(s)
foll	Follow(s)/Following
G st	Garter stitch
inc	Increase
k	Knit
kfb	Knit into the front and back of a stitch
kfbf	Knit into the front, back and front of a stitch
k2tog	Knit 2 stitches together
k3tog	Knit 3 stitches together
kwise	As if to knit
LH	Left hand
MC	Main colour
M1	Work as M1L
M1L	Make 1 Left; pick up strand between the two needles from the front to back with the tip of left needle, knit into the back of this stitch
M1R	Make 1 Right; pick up strand between the two needles from back to front with the tip of left needle, knit into the front of this stitch
M1P	Work as M1LP
M1LP	Make 1 Left Purlwise; pick up strand between the two needles from front to back with the tip of left needle, purl into the back of this stitch
M1RP	Make 1 Right Purlwise; pick up strand between the two needles from back to front with the tip of left needle, purl into the front of this stitch
patt	Pattern
PM	Place marker
p	Purl
pfb	Purl into the front and back of a stitch
pwise	As if to purl
p2tog	Purl 2 stitches together
rem	Remain(s)/Remaining
rep	Repeat
rev St st	Reverse Stocking stitch (stockinette): purl on RS rows, knit on WS rows
RH	Right hand
RS	Right side of fabric
sl	Slip
sl1yo	Bring working yarn between needles to the front of work as if to purl. Slip next st pwise without working, allowing working yarn to create a yarnover on needle as you work the next st. These 2 strands will be worked as a brk or brp in following row/round.
s2kpo	Slip 2 stitches together knitwise, knit next stitch, pass slipped stitches over
sk2po	Slip 1 stitch knitwise, knit next 2 stitches together, pass slipped stitch over
ssk	Slip 2 stitches knitwise one at a time, knit together through the back loops
sssk	Slip 3 stitches knitwise one at a time, knit together through the back loops
ssp	Slip 2 stitches knitwise one at a time, purl together through the back loops
SM	Slip marker
st(s)	Stitch(es)
St st	Stocking stitch (stockinette): knit on RS rows, purl on WS rows
tbl	Through the back loop
tog	Together
wyib	With yarn held in back of work
wyif	With yarn held in front of work
w&t	Wrap and turn: **RS:** Bring working yarn between needles from back to front as if to purl. Sl next st pwise from left hand needle to right. Bring working yarn back between needles from front to back. Sl same st pwise back to left hand needle. Turn. **WS:** Bring working yarn between needles from front to back as if to knit. Sl next st pwise from left hand needle to right. Bring working yarn back between needles from back to front. Sl same st pwise back to left hand needle. Turn.
WS	Wrong side of fabric
yo	Yarn over needle and into working position

Techniques

Pom Pom Tutorials
Backwards loop cast on: pompommag.com/tutorials
Crochet provisional cast on: http://bit.ly/2czeJh4
Kitchener stitch: http://bit.ly/2czgoD3
Long-tail cast on: pompommag.com/tutorials
Wrap and turn: pompommag.com/tutorials

Cable cast on: Insert right hand needle between first and second sts on left hand needle. Wrap yarn and pull through as if knitting. Do not slip sts from left hand needle. Place new st over left hand needle (1 st cast on). Repeat as directed by pattern.

Conceal wrap: Work to wrapped st, and pick up strand of yarn wrapped around base of st from the RS. Work wrapped st together with picked up strand in a k2tog (RS) or p2tog (WS).

THE END

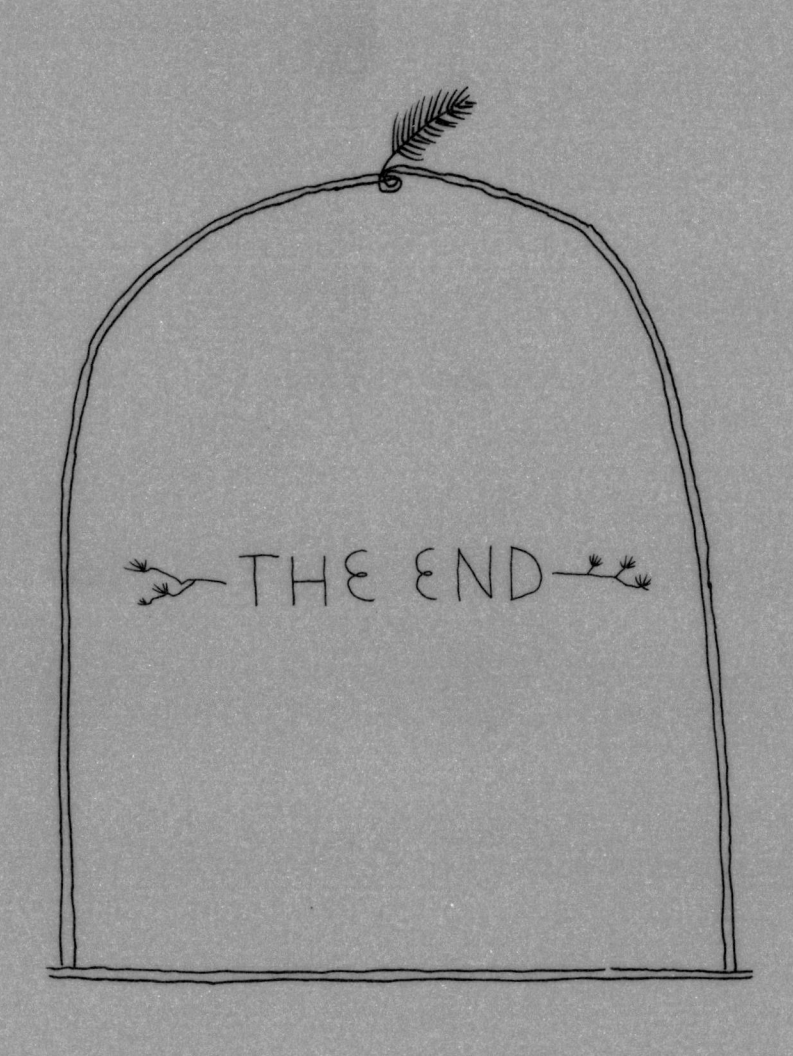

THE END